OBJECTL

A book series about the hidden lives of ordinary things.

Series Editors:

Ian Bogost and Christopher Schaberg

Advisory Board:

Sara Ahmed, Jane Bennett, Johanna Drucker, Raiford Guins, Graham Harman, renée hoogland, Pam Houston, Eileen Joy, Douglas Kahn, Daniel Miller, Esther Milne, Timothy Morton, Nigel Thrift, Kathleen Stewart, Rob Walker, Michele White.

In association with

BOOKS IN THE SERIES

waste

BRIAN THILL

BLOOMSBURY ACADEMIC
NEW YORK • LONDON • OXFORD • NEW DELHI • SYDNEY

BLOOMSBURY ACADEMIC
Bloomsbury Publishing Inc
1385 Broadway, New York, NY 10018, USA
50 Bedford Square, London, WC1B 3DP, UK

BLOOMSBURY, BLOOMSBURY ACADEMIC and the Diana logo are trademarks
of Bloomsbury Publishing Plc

First published 2015
Reprinted 2017, 2018

Bloomsbury Publishing Inc does not have any control over, or responsibility for, any
third-party websites referred to or in this book. All internet addresses given in this
book were correct at the time of going to press. The author and publisher regret
any inconvenience caused if addresses have changed or sites have ceased to
exist, but can accept no responsibility for any such changes.

Thill, Brian.
Waste/Brian Thill.
pages cm – (Object lessons)
Includes bibliographical references and index.
ISBN 978-1-62892-436-7 (pbk.: alk. paper) 1. Refuse and refuse disposal–
Philosophy. 2. Refuse and refuse disposal–Moral and ethical aspects. 3. Personal
belongings–Psychological aspects. 4. Waste (Economics) I. Title.
TD791.T45 2015
363.7–dc23
2015013080

ISBN: PB: 978-1-6289-2436-7
ePub: 978-1-6289-2438-1
ePDF: 978-1-6289-2439-8

Series: Object Lessons

Typeset by Deanta Global Publishing Services, Chennai, India
Printed and bound in Great Britain

To find out more about our authors and books visit www.bloomsbury.com
and sign up for our newsletters.

To Olivia, always

We are not in the least afraid of ruins.

BUENAVENTURA DURRUTI

One must work with the trash, pit it against itself.

**PHILIP K. DICK,
IN A LETTER TO STANISLAW LEM**

I'm an optimist, I think. But there it is, rotting.

EILEEN MYLES

CONTENTS

CONTENTS

1 THE BEACH THAT SPEAKS

In Paul Valéry's *Eupalinos; or The Architect*, Socrates is walking alone on the beach. He stumbles upon an obscure object, polished and white. He can't figure out what it is or where it came from. As he later tells Phaedrus, the seashore is a special kind of wasteland, a place of derelict things, a gathering-zone for all the detritus of a great and eternal struggle:

> This frontier between Neptune and Earth, ever disputed by those rival divinities, is the scene of the most dismal and most incessant commerce. That which the sea rejects, that which the land cannot retain, the enigmatic bits of drift; the hideous limbs of dislocated ships, black as charcoal, and looking as though charred by the salt tempests from the transparent pasture-grounds of Proteus' flocks; collapsed monsters, of cold deathly hues; all the things, in short, that fortune delivers over to the fury of the

shore, and to the fruitless litigation between the wave and beach, are there carried to and fro; raised, lowered; seized, lost, seized again according to the hour and the day; sad witnesses to the indifference of the fates, ignoble treasures, playthings of an interchange as perpetual as it is stationary. . . .

The enigmatic object Socrates finds on the shore is inscrutable but—for that very reason—captivating; he can't even be sure whether it is the product of nature or of human craft. Bewildered by its mysterious origins, status, and purpose, bested by it, he hurls the unknowable thing back into the sea.

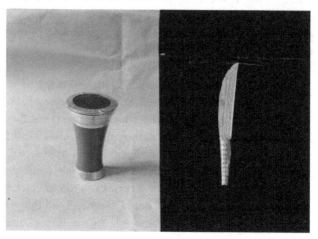

FIGURE 1

Socrates' problem is the problem of waste. The world around us is filled with charred remnants and scattered filth in too many forms; too diffuse, of every size and shape and smell, ugly and unwieldy, born of every age and temperament. It seeps into every crevice, floats down every grime-choked street, pools and piles and decays in every corner of every home and city and patch of wilderness. And there is always so much more of it than we can ever hope to study. A beachcomber of the 1990s might have stumbled upon The Nikes of Queets, washed ashore after the Great Shoe Spill, when entire shipping containers filled with high-priced shoes spilled into the sea before their cargo slowly made its way to the beaches of the Pacific Northwest. Recent hikers of Mt. Everest will find piles of earlier explorers' accumulated trash that they are now obligated to bring down with them upon their return, alongside their own equipment and their noble fatigue. There is no human-made object so well traveled, so ambient, as waste. It fills the oceans and the highest peaks. Our waste lays thick blankets of our chemical age across the entire planet, into every rocky outcropping, to the bottom of every sea's floor, nestling in the trees and bogs and pools of the world. It's in the air, in the water, in yard sales brimming with kitsch, in houses stuffed to the rafters with rubbish, in outer space, spreading out in invisible clouds of toxic chemicals, and piling up in immense mountains of garbage stacked in trash-bricks below ground at Fresh Kills or Puente Hills or a thousand other dump sites. The soil itself is part of a new geology, as the beaches have been remade into plastiglomerate, their sands mingled with the pulverized microplastics of our petroleum age. The genes of sea creatures that ingest these incredibly small fragments of our trash are mutating. Geologists have now begun to study "technofossils" and the sedimented debris-layers of our vast compressed cities, so immense and consequential that they now constitute part of the geological and planetary record. With our waste we have reordered space and place, reshaping them in its image the world over. But many of us are fortunate or foolish enough to tend not to *feel* the world in this way most of the time. In places, the air still seems breathable, trees manage to seem vibrant and green, squirrels appear happy and filled with energy. Even so, if one of humankind's desires has been to put its stamp on the world, waste is the most compelling and universal way in which it has accomplished its mission. Every landscape is a trashscape. This not only transforms the world into one vast and unevenly distributed trash heap; it changes, in ways that might not even be perceptible to us, our sense of self and humanity in the world. As the sociologist Zygmunt Bauman notes, we have colonized it all with our waste and the elaborate processes that produced it, creating human waste and wasted human lives all along globalization's dirty path; and now we must consider where these waste-products, living and dead, could go next; or what it means for us if there really is nowhere else to go. There is no path past the wastes we've made. Reading Bauman reminds you that we have built for ourselves, and the future, an enormous nest made of our own civilizational excrement.

If you wanted to consider an object more resistant to capture, you would be hard pressed to find one. Waste challenges our ability to adjust our contemplation of it to the proper scale. Every thought about waste seems much too big or much too small. So the temptation is to want to encompass everything: to name and honor and linger over every bit of crud and driftwood; to let the term spread out and away from us like an oil slick to encompass the wastage of the entire planet, the extermination of entire cultures and peoples, the wastes that make and unmake empires; massive waste and minuscule, visible and invisible, chemical pollutants,

FIGURE 2

decaying food, everything clogging up the gray air and the brown water and the trash-covered land.

Among all these scattered objects, I am less interested in the decayed remnants of grandiose ancient monuments than with some of the other classes of waste that have supplanted them in our age: buried video games; the slow leak of decaying plutonium miles below ground; the plastic bag caught in the tree; the accumulated wreckage in our attics, barns, and living rooms; the satellite debris hurling through space. These are the markers laid down on the bet we have made with futurity. In the end the final disposition of our water bottles, our websites, our Happy Meal toys, and our bombs will say as much about time and humanity as the fates of the Statue of Liberty, the Great Wall, or the Coliseum will. In *Pleasure of Ruins*, Rose Macaulay writes with deep erudition and affection about the pleasure that classical ruins have given to people for centuries. Exemplified by the sentiments of Diderot and other Romantic admirers of antiquity's enduring fragments, these types of ruins seem to possess the power to wring powerful emotions and feelings from us: the thrill or desperation or sorrow that attends contemplation of vanished ages, or the shock of situating ourselves within the endless rushing stream of time. We believe we have some emotional attachment to the stories about humanity that the tumbled stones of ancient ruins seem to tell. But I am much more drawn to what Gilda Williams has characterized as the difference between the "ruin" that captivated Diderot and melancholics everywhere and its lowly counterpart, the "derelict." The ruin is a thing of wonder and Romantic grandeur; it inspires poetry, whereas the derelict seems to cry out for burial or demolition. It is the difference between a majestic crumbling beauty and an eyesore, a hazard, or a nuisance. For my part, I understand the derelict as that immense underclass of things that have much more quickly or surreptitiously fallen outside of visibility and desire in our time: the indifferent, the lost, the wayward, the leaking, the ugly, the truly abject and unwanted—all the meddlesome waste caught in the cracks between the things we've built up in our minds as meaningful and majestic. In every new and shiny object of our age, and in every tiny and seemingly insignificant object of attention, I cannot help but see its erasure, or imagine its rusting, splintered, discarded husk decaying somewhere in the near future. I cannot seem to see objects embedded in their present time and space; they always carom off the edges of the present and into the past and the future, constantly, for me, whether I wish to see them this way or not. So this book is not a systematic environmentalist polemic, an academic monograph on the histories of sanitation, or a political manifesto (three of my favorite things). It is instead a meandering ramble through an idiosyncratic handful of the collapsed monsters and enigmatic bits of drift that have caught my eye, as a dirty penny on the street might not interest a hundred people passing by before it finally finds someone who covets it. This book is meant for the *flâneurs* of filth, those who like to wrestle with the cinders and rummage around in the midden heap haphazardly. For some of us, a lofty ruin does nothing; we are for the ramshackle and the derelict every time.

Like the maddening object that Socrates finds and then tosses away, all the derelict objects of our immense object-worlds, whether they are busted pianos, sandwich wrappers, egg cartons, unfashionable bathroom tiles, or corrugated coffee-cup sleeves, are likewise the playthings of an endless litigation, tossed between desire and detritus, waste and want. So if waste is this book's object, its real subjects are *desire* and *time*, because the things we call our waste exist in an interzone between two states of mind and two structures of feeling about the glittering, shattered object-worlds we have built around ourselves. These relics float between the poles of desire and discard. More than mere trash or hazard, a better way to think about waste is to think of it as the unsatisfactory and temporary name we give to the affective relationships we have with our unwanted objects. Waste is the expression of expended, transmuted, or suspended desire, and is, therefore, the *ur*-object. To talk about waste is to talk about every other object that has ever existed or will ever exist. Conversely, to talk about any object at all is to gesture toward its ultimate annihilated state. Waste is every object, plus time.

In Chris Jordan's photographs of the desiccated bodies of dead albatrosses, we see an assemblage of what might at first appear to be outcasts from some Rauschenberg installation gone to seed. Their innards (or what had once been their innards before they had been turned inside out by death) are filled to bursting with our plastic waste, and everything has come spilling out of them like candy from a busted piñata. From inside their decomposing bodies we see an astonishing array of brightly colored and elaborately shaped fragments of plastic. Many of the birds mistook these small chunks of our trash for food and scooped them up in the region of the Great Pacific garbage vortex, or their mothers had fed the plastic to them long before they were able to swallow garbage on their own. In the birds' exploded insides we see the specific, individualized limits of the body burden that our plastisphere offers up in tantalizing morsels to hapless animals.

What makes Jordan's photographs particularly arresting is that they capture the birds' decaying process just at the moment when the last vestiges of the animal that once consumed these shards of our waste are beginning to vanish. We can see the trace outlines of a skull here, an assortment of thin rib bones there, but in general the basket of bright plastic trash appears to be nestled comfortably in a bolus of tiny exploded feathers, as if some trash artisan had left his wares out among the island rocks for passersby to contemplate and enjoy. But if the remnants of the dead birds' bodies are often hard to discern clearly, as time and the environment eat away at every part of the bird that was not artificial, the cornucopia of plastic objects embedded in their entrails likewise appears to be visible and yet maddeningly indistinct, familiar and yet inscrutable, as the obscure object on the shore was for Valéry's Socrates. Most of the visible objects are clearly human-made and plastic, but it's often difficult to decipher exactly what each object used to be when it was part of something we thought we needed. The sense one gets in staring for a long time into these nests of plastic is that they belong to us and yet feel apart from us, because they constitute the planetary debris field we have scattered so thoroughly and minutely that it's hard to find anything particularly spectacular or notable in it. It is one of the many instances when seemingly minor trash demonstrates its immense strength and durability, having reached every corner of our planet and troubled or killed so many of the

FIGURE 3

things it touches. This small gathering of gutted birds points us toward all those that were never photographed but met similar fates, the ones who choked to death silently on some bright crag, or fell into the sea with a nearly invisible splash.

Jordan is certainly not unique in providing documentary images of the specific tolls that our garbage takes on the animal kingdom. But these images in particular are engrossing for another reason. If they chronicle the moments in time when the individual dead birds seem to be losing their essential birdness, they also capture a key moment in the incredibly long life cycles of the plastics that killed them. The new plastic collectives gathered here appear to us in their own moment of transition. As our trillion pieces of indigestible plastic spread daily across the globe, they flicker in and out of view, appearing in our storm drains or rolling down our streets before being dumped out to sea. We may see them bobbing in the water briefly before they drift away or sink, and are forgotten. But here, in the moments Jordan captures, we are looking at where the scattered waste objects have reassembled once more into a mass, to pass through, in a bundle, the bodies they have destroyed. These shards of ours form a temporary congregation in the bodies of the living before being excreted to the elements once more, and Jordan's photographs mark this moment of passage, arresting it in time, as the wind begins to carry away the feathers and bones that are all that remains of the birds brought down by our desire for convenience. These images shine a light on those spaces hidden from view most of the time, like the elephant graveyards of old. In looking at them we are gazing upon the open graves of our waste-glutted messengers. The birds have devoured waste from hundreds of people who will never meet and never know of each other's existence, but the birds' innards provide an alternate gathering space for reordering the wastescapes of human activity on a much longer time scale and across new geographical imaginaries. In performing this deadly service for us these birds become a temporary nexus for a scattered humanity, a morbid meeting-place where our collective waste is their last meal.

This vertiginous feeling of looking down into the innards of plastic-choked birds is not unlike the feeling of gazing down from the subway platform into the wet brown spaces of the train tracks to see what we find there, in the dark places where fetid puddles of assorted liquids mingle with grungy water bottles, soda cans, expired MetroCards, flattened bits of mildewed paper, and other objects smudged and smashed beyond recognition. Unlike the city above us, the platform offers few vistas, and the conventions of city life militate against most engagements with the other assembled strangers. The occasional rat skitters across the filth, emerging out of some invisible passageway somewhere beneath us before vanishing again into another equally obscure tunnel just before the train's approach. On the platform I always find myself staring down into that rust-brown garbage pooled down around the tracks. It's nasty, and I can't look away.

If you take one of those trains down to the end of the line at Flatbush Avenue and make your way south, well past Kings Highway, past the inlet of Jamaica Bay and all the way to Barren Island, a talon of land at the bottom of Brooklyn, eventually you reach the almost hidden entrance to Dead Horse Bay. This is where they used to dump the horse bones and glassware of an earlier era of New York sanitation before the need to find much larger dumping-grounds further afield became necessary. Birds fly overhead; the waves arrive quietly from the sea. In comparison to the modern-day municipal trashscapes available to the average wastehound, Dead Horse Bay is much smaller and far more unsettling, particularly on an overcast morning when no other person is in sight, and the metropolis of New York itself has almost completely vanished from the horizon. Even the long road out to the bay is clean and desolate; it has the quiet emptiness of the roads that surround regional airports and minimum-security research facilities. You are allowed to be here, more or less, but nothing in the landscape welcomes you, and the incessant green quiet of the area seems to repel all but the most stubborn and disconsolate wanderers. Once you have found the entrance area there is still the matter of getting to the beach-dump itself, which is entirely hidden from roadside view by dense thickets of foliage running along the coast road in each direction. Where most of life is lived in an urban setting, the sudden approach of an edgeland like this requires a certain furtive energy and a recklessness to explore. If you did not know where to find the trail you would probably never notice the trailhead tucked behind a demure band of orange plastic netting. The path to the water zigzags through a distressing tangle of trees, weeds, and scrubland. If you are in a certain frame of mind, walking through it feels like the opening gambit of a horror film, a maze of death far from civilization, where rabbits nibble on the dewy grass, miniature clouds of mosquitoes hover in wait, and you cannot see the road or the water or anything above you or anything inside the low canopy that hems you in and compels you to quicken your pace. It is the kind of place where a fevered imagination might plant a madman or a ghastly relic emerging out of the green fog to devour you in terrible silence. A place that feels so empty and uninhabited should not also feel so manicured, and this places the trail somewhere out of joint with most other places you might visit on days when you are not looking for old garbage.

But eventually, if the monsters have not carried you off, you arrive at the beach, and if it is high tide and the wind is low and steady you feel that you might have stumbled into a separate desolation. A dry-docked derelict boat, a spavined tree festooned with a crown of dangling bottles swaying in the breeze, the beach littered north to south with a bewildering jumble of detritus. On my initial visit the first thing I saw at the water's edge was an enormous horseshoe crab, its tail gently swaying back and forth, thin and precise as the needle on a metronome, the enormous bulbous mass of its body peeking out from the top of the water like the moist gray skull of a giant. I had never seen a horseshoe crab out in the world before this moment, and the fact of this fossil's living existence momentarily made me forget that I had come to this beach to look at its garbage, at what was supposedly dead there and not at what was alive. In recent decades, the bay has become a mecca for local trashhounds, as evidenced by the ornate trash-trees, waste-temples, signs, markers, and bone-and-bottle tableaux. Once you have found what you believe to be an old intact bottle, it doesn't take much to confirm whether or not this is actually true. There are specific manufacture marks on most bottles produced in the past two centuries, and once you begin to spend some time

FIGURE 4

digging around in them, you get better at quickly identifying certain obvious markers: the presence or absence of screw tops (most of the truly old ones used cork stoppers), its color (period of manufacture can often be readily identified by way of the dominant glass colors), or where the seams are that join the various pieces of manufactured glass to form the bottle itself, since the processes of mass-producing glass bottles eventually required more reliance on pre-formed molds.

Looking into these features, you soon discover that the wastes piled up here are from the historical period of its use as a major dumping-ground in the age of horse and glass, but also from every other period since, especially from the very recent past. This is no mere disposal site to be looted by collectors of antique glass, but is in fact better understood as a dispersal site for its much more recent denizens. Having long since ceased to be an official disposal site, it has taken on a new and much less advertised second life as a place to leave certain types of waste, as much as it is a place to find old waste to bring home for use in your cabinets of curiosity. On one visit I came across no fewer than half a dozen brand-new Log Cabin syrup bottles casually tossed into the near surf by some unknown party, and it is now common to find relatively recent examples of semi-attractive ornate glass bottles, faux-vintage ceramics, and toys that appear to be antiquated scattered here and there. What motives drive this practice? To salt the earth with a new layer and a new era of glass, a project of historical continuity? Or something more nefarious: A perverse desire to dupe the unwitting visitor who arrives seeking old treasures and returns home with a chipped saucer from Ikea? There is a certain kind of glee in thinking about someone being hoodwinked by the artifacts you've strewn along the beach, even more so if you've found old things there yourself. Perhaps the practice is not malicious, but merely playful: this is the beach where glass and pretty kinds of garbage go, so here is some more of it. Clearly most of the new items here aren't items that were in fact litter, as we might see with a carelessly tossed beer bottle or soiled diaper. These dishes and toys and bottles of interesting shape and size and color were brought here relatively recently, lugged here on purpose to be left behind for others to find, to be mistaken for the waste of ages past, and for other inscrutable purposes.

In this way, Dead Horse Bay is much more than a mere historical dumping-ground that has acquired enough age to lend it a renewed antiquarian interest in our plastic age. At this point in its history, the site has also become a peculiar kind of communication hub between its disparate visitors, with garbages old and new as their communicating technology. It is less a site that invites pilfering or leaving something behind than one that invites us to communicate via trashspeak with those who are absent, those who came before us, but also those who will come after. Here at Dead Horse, waste becomes a playful but earnest mechanism to speak back to the dead; to assert the continuity of our disjointed present with times before, when horse's bones were dumped in great piles here to be cleansed by the tides or gobbled up by the mud; and to behave on the beach with an eye toward the times to come, when the brand-new items we've tossed out there for whatever idiosyncratic purposes are actually part of our own manufactured past. It is in this respect the antithesis of practical sanitation-thinking that necessitates some of the largest modern dumps, like Freshkills on the east coast or Puente Hills out west (just down the hill from where I lived as a small child), where the need and the desire is simply to manage the unceasing mess of modern life, to entomb and erase our daily trash. People come to Dead Horse for a congress with the objects of the past, and find, mingled among them, the objects of our present, coyly deposited there to fool the hapless or to initiate new conversations between the wastes of different days and different ages. It has become a place to leave a relic for the near or far future, a shore whose message is not inside a bottle, but is the discarded bottle itself.

2 TRASH FAMILIARS/ TABFLAB

Dead Horse Bay is one of the few places where we can differentiate between what we might call *volitional* waste (relatively new and common tea saucers and ceramic figurines meant to be found and cherished anew) and the average discarded beer bottle. It is one of the few places where there is more than just mere litter, where it would be more accurate to describe the acts on the beach as littering-with-intent. The amount of effort given to throwing something away in this particular fashion stands in sharp contrast to the work of the everyday litterbug, whose actions seem cavalier and obnoxious by comparison. Ordinary litter reminds us that we think about the objects we've casually tossed aside about as much, or as deeply, as we think about the nature and provenance of those objects before they arrive in our hands—that is to say, hardly at all. We tend to use the things that come to us and then discard what is left, and give little thought to their previous lives or afterlives. And yet when we see someone else toss a piece of trash on the ground, we seem to act as if it offends us.

By contrast, mere litter is a special category of waste because its existence depends more than anything else on individualized indifference. The indifference engine that drives litter is the flip side of desire. It's the waste we could not bring ourselves to care even a little bit about, when we had, just moments before, cared about some part of the thing we're throwing out very much: the potato chips in the unwanted bag or the gum inside the tossed wrapper. One of the most familiar landmarks in the terrain of litter is the overflowing public garbage can, a common site in heavily trafficked and insufficiently funded public areas. Understood as a zone of waste-feeling, the overstuffed bin, unlike the simple piece of trash thrown anywhere on the street, indicates to us that the line between desire and discard is often a fluid and malleable one, and that it is possible for us to consider our relationship to personal waste as neither the bad citizenship of absolute disregard for the commons, nor the relentless mindset of the dedicated eco-warrior whose annual refuse can fit inside a single jar. Somewhere between these two we find the special phenomenon of modern times where waste is tossed or laid in the vicinity of a disposal site; where we see intent-to-dispose. It is no coincidence that this is most commonly seen on clogged city streets in the form of individual, single-use coffee cups or beverage containers. Our harried lives as members of the modern mochatariat are enmeshed in capital flows, where some of us are being trained to consider vague "responsibilities" toward our fellow humans, communities, and planet as consisting chiefly of making the effort to throw things in the right recycling bin, or to pick up the missed wad of trash and put it in its "proper" place, to be carted off by someone else and forgotten forever. The caffeinated classes must have their desires and needs satisfied, and then we must add our cups to the tumbling heap spilling out onto the ground and into the street, as we wonder in passing why some sanitation worker doesn't hurry up and get all of this mess out of the way. The omnipresence of the urban cup mountain speaks to the effort to appear to be conscious of some notion of proper places for waste and proper places free of them, although it isn't something we have the time or the desire to get too worked up about. There are, after all, so many other things we need to get done.

The coffee-cup mountain also calls to mind Jeffrey Inaba/C-Lab's *Trash Mandala*, a brightly colored, incredibly detailed art piece that renders the "hydration compulsion" of our time into a quasi-religious mythological tableau that chronicles our endless thirst for bottled water pilfered from the common lands. It conjures a world in which millions of ravenous affluent people, desperate for a few ounces of water, gobble it up and dispose of its containers, over and over and over again, never satiated, always filled with an unquenchable thirst that only millions of individual-serving name-brand bottles of water can even begin to satisfy; as if every hour of every day, in places where clean water is readily available for prepackaged consumption, we who buy water by the handful were always on the verge of shriveling up and blowing away. Water has become the necessity that we have decided must also generate truly incredible volumes of waste. If we have reached the age of peak oil, then we have also reached the age of peak plastic and peak individualism; and yet, like Tantalos, we keep clamoring for more.

Last winter, after the final leaf fell from the tree nearest my kitchen window, I spotted a plastic bag coiled in its thin branches, a common enough site wherever barren trees and a steady supply of litter obtain. These wispy daemons exist

FIGURE 5

in all seasons, but late autumn and early winter seem to be the time of their greatest flourishing. The next day, it was still there; and the next day, and the next. Through weeks of howling winds and rain and, eventually, ice and snow, the bag clung to its perch. And then one day several months later, after having trusted in it being there every day, immovable, my trash familiar was gone.

Generally, we expect all of this individualized and uncollected waste to be mobile, wayward, like the infamous bag in *American Beauty* or Ramin Bahrani's *Plastic Bag* (breathlessly narrated by Werner Herzog). At the same time, we hope or expect that properly collected waste is housed, "secure," as at Freshkills, where everything looks green and tamped down for a good long while, or so they hope. But waste is also an orphan object. It can often be found existing somewhere outside of both the free-floating state and entombment, at least for a time. Sometimes it lodges. It begins to establish itself in the neighborhood; it starts to accumulate squatter's rights. It is clearly garbage but it isn't going away as garbage is supposed to. The trash familiar troubles the line between our endlessly transient waste, blown here and there, and our cold storage. It threatens to become a fixture. The humble trash familiar is one way to see how wastes much larger and more dangerous than itself likewise respect no boundaries; they create their own lines of flight and vectors; they spread their fetor far from home, because in truth they have no home, in the same way that all undesired things lack a home. We should read the plastic bag hibernating in the tree as a sign for all the invisible wastes that lodge themselves in unwanted places, like a chicken bone stuck in the throat.

The world begins to feel trash-filled and inescapable. There must be cleaner, sleeker spaces, places that are bright and shiny and free of mold, mildew, and rust. You turn away from the window view of the billowing bag outside to the comforts of your computer, where the emails, chats, DMs, tabs, windows, pages, faves, documents, feeds, and streams continue to pile up like cars crashing into each other inside an endless fog. If the cups and bottles outside get crushed and the bags are shredded to pieces by the wind and rain, this digital debris becomes yet another unsettled wasteland to wander through. It sometimes presents itself to us in a way that can deceive us into thinking it is a world somehow dramatically different from all the trashscapes outside in meatspace, but of course it isn't.

For many of us in the digital age, it is a time of endlessly cascading microdesires, our wants and needs constantly refreshed, updated, streaming. The flood of things to keep or discard complicates our notions of interest and attention, which were already strained. Online it is even easier to feel the tidal pull of what Yves Citton describes as the new ecology of attention, where it is no longer simply about what we as individuals pay attention to (I may watch the rat on the train tracks, while another commuter turns away in disgust), but about the problem of transindividual attention. We log on and not only have our attention turned toward the great incomprehensible mass of news, gossip, information, and trivia, but do so in spaces that push us toward paying attention to what others are paying attention to at the same time. The lone beachcomber may have only her own thoughts and interests to guide her wanderings among the horse bones and antique bottles, but online she is drawn to a more vast menagerie, and to all the people moving through it in their collective-individual way. Unlike the view of the perched bag from the window, the view into the windows of digital spaces devours the present and the future alike; it pushes us toward a maximization of time as infinitely fungible, which is to say toward fantasy. For some of us, despite this fantasy of time's plasticity, there is pleasure and joy involved in this endlessly accumulated tabflab; in having so many friends and acquaintances, in discovering so many things, in being so plugged in; in swimming with the current of a vast and turbulent river of collective attention that just keeps getting larger and larger, and becomes a sea.

For this reason, and because I have seen so much waste everywhere else I looked that was not on a screen, I gave up on achieving Inbox Zero. I have come to accept it as a byproduct of the modern condition, where hundreds of objects and ideas and people compete for our constantly stretched attention. No matter how many of them we get to—and we are nothing if not active and productive—there are always so many more left by the wayside: articles we had intended to read; essays to write that molder half-formed in file folders; rabbit-holes of links and tabs and Tumblrs we always intended to cut a path through as soon as we had the time; posts and tweets and blogrolls and feeds to read, share, save, or forget. As precious and intriguing as these artifacts of modern life seem under certain conditions, they invariably transform into waste when they overtake us, when there's no hope of sifting through all of them and giving them the attention we think they need or deserve. But these digital barrens aren't quite like the piles of old-style material trash we send away from us as quickly as possible. They are, or have the potential to be, deep repositories of personal and collective history and memory, even if they are only occasionally used and only occasionally important. The rest of the time they sit, ignored, decaying into the silence of the expired fave, the deleted post, and the creeping link rot that sometimes seems to engulf every mildly aged space in our online world.

It would be easy to treat this as just a species of the overabundance of the object-world we've always inhabited, no different from the unread stacks of newspapers and *New Yorker*s, or the piles of books to read or the loads of laundry to be washed, or the groceries or the backlog of all of our work. And in a certain material sense, it remains the same. Just because I have forty tabs open or seventeen half-written documents or posts on my computer—rather than having them spread out on the floor in front of me—doesn't make them any less material or any less real. They are as earthbound as anything half-buried in the sand, and subject to the same material pressures. Digital waste is not freed from the realities of material existence. Just like the coffee we drink, its ongoing production consumes immense energy, labor, resources, time, and space, just as all the proliferating garbage of the pre-digital ages did and continues to do. As such, it's inextricably bound to social, political, and economic crises, just as our material waste has always been. But these digital wastespaces are also radically different. The desire for things like Inbox Zero or the calls to simplify your life or to pare down your digital footprint (as if it's somehow separate from your life in general these days) seem to miss something incredibly rich and important about how our modern lives actually work. The tendency of tabflab, fave-holes, document dumps, and other digital detritus to present itself as more expansive and "clean" to us means that it can also serve as a mechanism for rethinking our relationships to waste, time, memory, and the self. Historically, our relationship to all the many discarded bits of our everyday material lives had been one of abjection and removal. Traditionally, trash, as soon as it's classified as such, is wiped from sight and often from memory, at least for those of us with reliable garbage service. We hope and assume, naïvely, that our unwanted scraps are carted off to some enormous invisible dump somewhere, and more or less erased from our daily lives forever. But as environmental philosopher Timothy Morton has argued, there is no imaginary "Away" to cling to anymore. Our collective mountains of rubbish located somewhere vaguely "out there" speak volumes about the kinds of willfully ignorant modern lives we're living, but unlike our digital wastelands, that accumulated garbage is generally left to its entombment, unloved and largely unconsidered by us, invisible and mostly forgotten. The more precarious your life is, of course, the less sustainable that fantasy of expulsion and removal. Every breath of toxic air you breathe, every drink of carcinogenic water, every handful of polluted soil, reminds us that our trash always comes back to us—just not always to *us*, specifically.

In "La Poubelle Agréée," his long essay about taking out the garbage, Italo Calvino describes the process of taking his household trash out to the curb for the garbage workers as the transformation of waste from the private to the public sphere. For Calvino, this is a kind of ritual gesture that reminds him of the importance and value of a social compact, or what others might just call civilization. It allows him to valorize the garbage workers who pick up the waste of everyone's individual lives of industrialized consumption and disposal. Garbage workers, he claims, are "emissaries of the chthonic world, gravediggers of the inanimate . . . heralds of a possible salvation beyond the destruction inherent in all production and consumption, liberators from the weight of time's detritus, ponderous dark angels of lightness and clarity." And yet elsewhere in the essay Calvino makes the much less sophisticated-sounding, but I think, far truer and more relevant claim that our trash is basically like our feces. As Calvino tells us, he takes out his trash every day not just out of a natural concern for hygiene or as an opportunity to rhapsodize about sanitation workers, but so that on waking up the following morning, he may begin his day fresh and new. Waste for him is a disgusting remnant of things we processed, and now want or need to expel, to separate from ourselves by policing what we believe to be the proper boundaries of our selves. This is how many of us feel about the objects of our abjection, as we offload to some vague "public" our private rubbish, and do so without giving further thought to it most of the time, over and over again. As Calvino says, this is a rite of purification, the abandoning of "the detritus of myself." Through this ritual, he confirms the need to separate himself from a part of what was once his, so that tomorrow, he says, "I can identify completely (without residues) with what I am and have." Waste thus signifies something more than just a certain stage of an object's life cycle; it is our specific affective relationship to an object that makes it "waste" in the first place. Once desire has been squeezed out of it, we're left with the waste products of those desires. The thing loses its thingness, and becomes something to eliminate. It is as if the real dread we feel about our own waste is not its undesirable and ignoble putrescence, but the creeping fear that its unwanted proximity to us somehow threatens to erase or disturb our very sense of ourselves as discrete bodies.

But on a more immediate level, waste really becomes something for someone else to eliminate *for* you; and it's not actually abandoned and scrubbed from the world, just from your world, more or less. It still ends up somewhere, but by then our Romantic sense of the fresh and unencumbered clean self has moved on in its repetitive cycle of consumption, discard, and identity. While this is a pattern of consumption and abandonment of which many of us are guilty, wastemaking doesn't only work that way anymore, at least where the seemingly cleaner digital detritus of our lives is concerned. We dispose of things all the time online: we close tabs—some of them—and windows after we finish reading them; we throw some old documents in the "trash can," and we delete any unwanted files. Depending on whom you're talking to, most chats eventually end; feeds and digital checklists occasionally get thoroughly cleaned. But more and more, they don't really get completely cleaned up, and you never really get ahead of any of it. How could we, in a world of transindividual attention, buried in the largeness of the ever-changing world and everyone else's ongoing attentions to it? This world of digital detritus piles up as quickly as we can consume it. In this way, the information age is making digital hoarders of all of us. We are compelled to hold on to more and more virtual things we do not have the time or energy or space for. I remember when it was just books that piled up before I could find the time to read them; now it's everything on my hard drive, everything in my feeds, everything in the cloud.

Without neglecting the serious ecological consequences of all of this digital life predicated on material extraction, this hoarding can in some ways also feel like a good thing. These digital midden-heaps are major aides to memory, to new forms of journal-keeping, self-discovery, and self-rediscovery.

They are, at least potentially, deep archives of many of the collective energies and ideas and exchanges that are bound to our specific personal and cultural moments in ways that our bothersome coffee-cup mountains don't seem to be. This is just one of the reasons why trite generational arguments about the horrors of the technological age don't hold up to scrutiny. The culture we've inherited—which created the automobile and the interstate and the suburbs and the strip mall and the 401(k)—chastises this new age, in which we spend huge chunks of time on our tablets and phones, where for the most part we're in active conversation and engagement with other human beings, an element that always gets neglected

FIGURE 6

in those disparagements. And what are the corresponding wastelands that each generation has created? Long before we continued the practice, the pre-digital generations irradiated huge chunks of the planet, plasticized the oceans and the biosphere, and littered the earth with the discarded remnants of decades' worth of cheap disposable goods. And yet it's the millennial age that's somehow described as acting frivolous and wasteful, when, in fact, recent history seems to indicate that many of us struggling to survive today are ourselves the waste products of an era of economic expansion that (as Bauman and so many others have reminded us) may be rapidly coming to a cataclysmic close.

In the meantime, we're drowning, or at least treading water, in our sea of information and in our ballooning social relations. If we're all familiar with FOMO (Fear of Missing Out) we're perhaps less familiar with what we might call FOTO (Fear of Throwing Out), but it's just as real and just as important. If FOMO was grounded in an anxiety that many of us felt in trying to keep pace with social media, online interaction, information and prestige economies, fear of throwing out is the other side of the coin. There are so many good websites, journals, articles, writers, artists, causes, issues, conversations, chats, tweets, feeds; so many good things that, even among the many that we do get to, it's not uncommon for us to feel a sort of residual attachment to them, even when we're supposedly through with them, or when their time or circumstance has passed us by. It's not an instant nostalgia for the conversation flood so much as a kind of wake that our frenetic lives create as we move through them. But this wake lingers in ways it hadn't for earlier generations. If earlier generations dusted off old photo albums or shoeboxes filled with letters, what's likely to happen now and in the future with our accumulated digital pasts? We still do our fair share of traditional material hoarding too, but people aren't going to suddenly quit caring about obsessing over the past just because we have devices that allow us access to mountains of digital information in an eternally streaming present. Those pasts, recent and distant, are just going to be accessed and integrated differently. The fear of throwing out predates the digital age, but it's more alive now than ever. With so many things to keep up with in the eternal present of our contemporary lives, we're having to become more and more sophisticated curators, not only of the things that are precious to us, but also of our daily process of emptying out our desires toward things over and over again, as ponderous as the sanitation worker who spends his days knee-deep in everyone else's muck.

What is that feeling of scrolling through old status updates, faves, and blog posts if not a richer memory aide than even the most diligent of old-world diarists ever produced? When you compare the stash of memory-objects that earlier generations clung to (even if they only dusted them off once a decade) to our relatively constant access to huge chunks of our lengthening digital lives, we soon realize that the old unread blog post, the old favorited tweet, the old chat thread, can summon up a whole host of memories of days, months, and years past, with all the associations and thoughts and ideas that come with it. These touchstones contain within them the same potential that Proust's madeleine possessed. Just because it's a tweet from a year ago from your friend doesn't mean that it doesn't have deep associational and historical value. We are reminded of what our friends said, about the kinds of things we thought were worth reading or listening to, the pet obsessions we had, the superficial fads and gossip topics, and the more enduring matters. As with all collections of partially discarded objects, these remnants don't even come close to communicating the fullness of our lives (even Proust could only try to begin to do so), but they persist in us and for us in a way that our weekly curbside material trash, hauled away and forgotten, never will. These are wastelands that are simultaneously sites of forgetting and remembrance, of desire and abandonment, available to us in ways that are fundamentally different from the object-worlds of our homes, where we gather what is supposed to be important to us, and the trash that we put out every single week.

By their very nature, these digital wastelands trouble the distinction between desire and abjection, past and present, and therefore, most importantly, between old selves and the new self that is constantly forming—not just in the streaming, proliferating present, but with the ongoing influences of the digital pasts that we drag along with us, wanted and unwanted all at once. Calvino had argued that sloughing off the things you're done with and making a clean break is a necessary daily process of life. But today, there is no simple "detritus of myself" to discard, not when we're enmeshed in the remnants of our ornate and overflowing mediated lives. There is no life or self anymore without the residues Calvino gleefully and deliberately tossed aside each day—thank god for that.

3 PIGS IN SPACE

Before I wanted to be an astronaut I wanted to drive a garbage truck. This would have been in the Reagan years, probably the last period when it was still relatively common for an American child to dream of floating among the stars. I had seen *The Right Stuff* and watched the space shuttle launches with an intense zeal and followed the space news and knew all about the teacher who was going into space. I had NASA patches and collectible stamp sets and 1/64-scale plastic models of spacecraft that I would assemble lovingly. I could name all the astronauts aboard the doomed shuttle *Challenger*. I knew the names of the planets and the major constellations; knew the colors of certain obscure outer moons; I knew a galaxy from a solar system, a quark from a quasar, a black hole from dark matter. I remember cavorting around the grounds of the space center in Huntsville, Alabama under the menacing clouds of an approaching storm, buoyant, in complete ecstasy. But before all of this I had been an even smaller child, looking out the window at the approaching dump truck, flabbergasted at its size and capabilities, fascinated by its slow and free movements up and down every block and away to some unknown place where everything it scooped up was spit back out again and hidden in some remote spot on earth. From an early age, outer space and garbage dumps fascinated me in equal measure as mysterious elsewheres, and they have been conjoined in my mind as twin passions ever since.

As J. R. McNeill says in his chapter on "Space Pollution," authorities have historically taken the view that space debris is too expensive to do much of anything to eradicate it. "And anyway," he adds wryly, "space is so big that there's room for space junk. Any industrialist would have said the same of the atmosphere 150 years ago." In the 1860s, he notes, Chicagoans believed Lake Michigan was large enough to absorb all their waste. People dumped for many years in the Black Sea and the Yellow Sea and other such places with the same belief. Time, he says, proved them wrong. McNeill's larger point is that we as a society have long been in the habit of finding somewhere relatively large and remote from the major wastemakers to dump all of our waste, only really beginning to worry about it after it was already creating an array of very serious problems: pollution, contamination, expansion, radiation, destruction. Nowadays, of course, we have companies like Lockheed Martin designing a "Space Fence" for the U.S. Air Force to track all of our deadly, proliferating space debris. In October of 2014, the *Georges Lemaître*—an Automated Transfer Vehicle named after the Jesuit priest, astronomer, and professor of physics responsible for proposing the theory of an expanding universe years before Edwin Hubble—saved the International Space Station and its six human inhabitants from a near-collision with space debris that, had it struck, would have inflicted catastrophic damage. The procedure was incredibly challenging. In their typically understated rhetoric, the European Space Agency stated afterwards, "This is the first time the Station's international partners have avoided space debris with such urgency." Set into orbit, untethered to the land or the sea, this minor debris, which would have been beneath notice or concern for most people if it were down here, assumes massive importance. Its velocity, not its size, is what propels it back into our collective consciousness as an agent of destruction. This scrap yard panic stands in sharp contrast to the slow violence that Rob Nixon and Robert Bullard have been analyzing for so long: the sewage leak, the cancer alley, the accumulated toxic filth that destroys lives slowly and surreptitiously, and therefore does not merit attention in a world where everyday suffering happens piecemeal, where only exploding spaceships would catch our eye.

The fact that there existed in the 1970s not one but two TV shows about space garbage tells you everything you will ever need to know about television, and about the 1970s. *Quark* (the 1970s space-trash show that *didn't* star Andy Griffith) was a short-lived sitcom that followed the banal and unfunny adventures of a multi-species gang assigned to collect garbage in deep space. Written by Buck Henry, whose adaptation of *The Graduate* had earned him an Academy Award in the previous decade, *Quark* was also one of the worst television shows of the 1970s, and that is saying something. "My mission," Captain Quark tells us in voiceover, "to boldly seek out grime and grit, to collect the uncollectable space baggie, to always leave the area cleaner than when I found it." Garbage, we are told, is the real "final frontier." Quark wears a giant UGSP (United Galaxy Sanitation Patrol) patch on his chest, emblazoned with its ignominious logo, a stuffed and tied garbage bag. While he encounters other ship commanders who've been busy keeping the galaxy safe by defeating Bloton brigades or stealing Gorgon defense plans, he's been helming his trash barge crewed with a ragtag bag of walking clichés and incredibly offensive stereotypical characters. The other commanders don't care about his garbage tales ("Oh, so you're in garbage," one of them says. "That must be very, uh . . . interesting"). They get assigned exciting missions while The Head, an enormous talking head responsible for directing mission control, assigns him only "Garbage" over and over again. The final episode of the series, which mercifully occurred in its first season, ends with a riff on *2001: A Space Odyssey*. The super-intelligent computer Vanessa threatens to render all of them obsolete. She has been put in total command of the ship and its crew, and will eventually try to kill Quark and send him to his death among his piles of space garbage. The crew finally manages to regain control over their putative computer overlord. In the final shot of the series, the malevolent computer is thrown out into the void of space as "Born Free" plays wistfully. It has become a floating piece of star dreck: never to be collected, never to be missed.

FIGURE 7

Even as it displays its own horribly dated and offensive take on transgender issues, masculine and feminine identity markers, and good taste, the show struggles, in its incredibly dull and unsophisticated way, to articulate something about the class snobbery that has always been associated with those who traffic in garbage. It would be foolish to look too deeply into a piece of dreck like *Quark* for a critique of this deep-seated animus, but at the same time, the show's constant riffing on the science fiction tropes of *Star Trek* and myriad other genre shows and films of the period highlights the generally unrealistic and dematerialized world-building of those science fiction staples it is attempting to mock. Just as many have lambasted Tolkien's world for seeming to exist without any actual political economy, so too were many of the cinematic science fiction works of the period unwilling or unable to devote anything other than perfunctory attention to the nature of labor, reproduction of material conditions of life, or modes of economic organization. They set their stories amidst worlds of want or worlds of plenty, but did not extend much beyond that level of set dressing. It's one thing to see battles of intergalactic importance waged where that intergalactic struggle for power and survival is the main crisis driving the plot; but placed alongside the mundane realism of garbage runs, many of these seemingly intense outer-space crises suddenly start to feel like so much genre bombast. If nothing else, at least the work that the *Quark* crew does feels vaguely real by comparison.

We see this scornful attitude toward waste almost everywhere that science fiction depends on displays of technological advancement and interstellar exercises of power, which was, and remains, the dominant method of distinguishing the worlds depicted in science fiction from our own. In the *Star Trek* episode "The Trouble with Tribbles," Scotty, the chief engineer, is having a drink with Lieutenant Chekov when Korax, a Klingon executive officer, launches into a venomous attack on the character of Captain Kirk and the starship *Enterprise*. He begins by talking trash about Earthers, who remind him of Regulan bloodworms.

Chekov is getting upset, but Scotty calms him down. Korax then qualifies his statement by stating emphatically that Captain Kirk is the only Earthman who doesn't remind him of a Regulan bloodworm, but he immediately qualifies this statement: "A Regulan bloodworm," he adds, "is soft and shapeless, but Kirk isn't soft. Kirk may be a swaggering, overbearing, tin-plated dictator with delusions of godhood, but he's not soft." An unrattled Scotty keeps Chekov from starting a fight over these insults, but then Korax takes things too far for Scotty to abide:

> KORAX: Of course I'd say that Captain Kirk deserves his ship. We like the *Enterprise*. We, we really do. That sagging old rust bucket is designed like a garbage scow. Half the quadrant knows it. That's why they're learning to speak Klingonese.
> CHEKOV: Mister Scott!
> SCOTT *[to Korax]*: Laddie, don't you think you should rephrase that?
> KORAX: You're right, I should. I didn't mean to say that the *Enterprise* should be hauling garbage. I meant to say that it should be hauled away *as* garbage.

At which point all hell breaks loose. As a young viewer, I could never quite understand what was so offensive about a garbage scow anyway. Later I'd come to recognize that sanitation is usually seen as a line of work that is looked down on not because it is unimportant, but because it's the job that places us most squarely back in the filth we would prefer to disavow. In rejecting our waste, we seek to reject everything associated with it. *Quark* mocks the false cleanliness of the worlds of *Star Trek* and elsewhere, and works like *Star Trek* reinforce that view, where the vision of the future must imagine smooth surfaces, lack of dirt, and orderliness as a precondition for civilizational advancement or survival, which requires getting into and out of constant messes of a very different kind, but to do so while looking good.

Trash functions as a convenient punch line, and not just in science fiction, but throughout popular culture as well. The ability to eliminate, contain, hide, or transcend landscapes of waste has been one of the most enduring visual and linguistic signifiers of traditional utopian science fiction (especially science fiction on film), whereas nearly every dystopia must embed its share of trash, filth, scunge, and wreckage. This is one crude way in which political economy and social organization was registered in a facile way in science fiction film and narrative, and why the visual field had been so important to establishing the general terrain in which particular science fiction stories were to be told. One of the genre markers of a perfectly achieved totalitarian future regime is in linking its technological advancement and its perceived "orderliness" to the cold sterility of a clean, waste-free vista. In its architectures, its social planning, its daily lives and customs, there remains something inhuman and soulless about it that is meant to alarm us, as H. G. Wells' unnamed Time Traveller was as soon as he stumbled upon the pastoral nightmare of the Eloi sunning themselves on the rocks while one of their own nearly drowns within arm's reach of them, and as their libraries of ancient books molder unread, reduced to useless dust.

Samuel R. Delany pointed out some of the ways that this visual and narrative field of traditional science fiction was leaving aside more relevant and textured depictions of the future, in particular, the future-worlds he categorizes under the broader rubric of "Junk City":

Junk City begins, of course, as a working class suburban phenomenon: think of the car with half its motor and three wheels gone which has been sitting out in the yard beside that doorless refrigerator for the last four years. As I kid I encountered the first signs of Junk City in the cartons of discarded military electronic components, selling for a quarter or 75 cents, all along Canal Street's Radio Row. But Junk City really comes into its own at the high tech moment, when all this invades the home or your own neighborhood: the coffee table with the missing leg propped up by the stack of video game cartridges, or the drawer full of miscellaneous walkman earphones, or the burned out building of the inner city, outside of which last year's $5,000 computer units are set out on the street corner for the garbage man (or whoever gets there first), because the office struggling on here for the cheap rent is replacing them with this year's model that does five times more and costs a third as much: here we have an image of techno chaos entirely different from the regimentation of Brave New World—and one that neither Huxley in the early '30s nor Orwell in the late '40s could have envisioned.

Those of us who grew up in environments where waste (ours and other people's) tended to accumulate in myriad ways see Junk City as a fundamentally realistic vision of the future—which, as we know, is really about our junk-strewn present. Junk City is another name for the favelas, the ghettoes, and the inner cities, the hood, the edgelands where all the detritus of consumer culture ends up as secondhand discard to form the spine and backdrop of a readymade Crobuzonic shantytown, unwelcome and mostly inescapable. This is what makes the talking, mobile trash can in Bruce Sterling's *Islands in the Net*, or the "kipple," or endless waste, that will eventually overtake the world in Philip K. Dick's *Do Androids Dream of Electric Sheep?* so memorable. In Dick's novel, rockets from earth are sent off-world to Mars with their payloads of cheap pulp sci-fi paperbacks and all the dirty kipple of earth, bursting out, unread, unloved. In Gene Wolfe's *Book of the New Sun*, the far-future guild of torturers makes its dismal residence inside the belly of an enormous repurposed spacecraft, the technological prowess of a golden age of civilization now long since vanished into the mists of time. In David Foster Wallace's *Infinite Jest*, a near-future America catapults its enormous overflows of garbage into the expropriated lands of Canada now known only as "the Great Concavity." In *Futurama* it's launched into space. In *Idiocracy*, the America of the future is drowning in its piles of garbage as society slouches toward a dimwitted consumerist Armageddon. And in Disney's *Wall-E*, Earthlings have left their garbage behind and taken their bloated selves to the stars, leaving behind a planet whose mountain ranges are the work of humankind's insatiable desire for junk. These and so many other examples indicate that the way we think about the relationship of waste to our visions of utopian or dystopian futures must reckon with the powerful resonance of Junk City as a guiding image for our age.

Much more than it did in bad 1970s' science fiction television or a significant portion of golden age science-fiction novels, waste and its impact have become a popular field for thinking about possible futures, a vehicle through which science fiction tries to work through its ambivalence about our desires to transcend the irreducible messiness of time, space, and mortality, as well as our simultaneous fears of being rendered obsolete in the new technological utopia. In Delany's body of work, as well as in Alfonso Cuarón's *Gravity*, Makoto Yukimura's manga series *Planetes*, Neill Blomkamp's *District 9*, and elsewhere, waste and its impact on humans and posthumans serves as a useful counterweight to the genre's own longstanding interests in exploring the limits of those gleaming futures, where some of the technocratic, political, and social problems of our age and the next have evidently been "solved," but only in the way that a street sweeper "solves" the problem of trash in the gutter—as a state always necessarily on the verge of returning to the disorder and mess of life. Exploded satellites, rusting carcasses of old space stations, burnted remnants, errant nuts and bolts tumbling at thousands of miles per hour through the silent reaches of space: all of these break up the tedium of a world that is not merely striving to eliminate human waste, but humans themselves. It is possible that the fascination with joining advanced technological, scientific, or civilizational developments and future history with something like waste is an indication that even the most utopian among us hold fast to longstanding beliefs about the fallibility of human nature. No matter how advanced the imaginary civilization, we often seem to account for the humanness within it through our messiness and our maddening, irreducible complexity; we still seem to be tethered to the dander and flatulence that somehow still signifies that which is human, even when we have fled the solar system, hacked our genes, developed AI and light-speed spaceships, and colonized the stars. Waste, trash, the dirty and unclean assert themselves in Cuarón, Philip K. Dick, Yukimura, and countless other instances as signs of the stubborn resistance to total order that advanced societies are supposed to be shepherding us toward. These imaginary worlds point us toward a future time (maybe far distant, maybe tomorrow) when, if we are not careful, we will have reached the point when humans themselves

FIGURE 8

will come to be seen as clunky and unwanted vestiges of a world mired for so long in the muck and debris of grimy and inefficient human endeavors. Perhaps our panic about our own filthiness, as much as our ambition and curiosity, is what has sent us running to the stars.

The hazardous trajectory of our seemingly minor debris in orbit makes it the one type of human-made waste that literalizes the threat of the eternal return. Things don't quite boomerang on earth as they do in orbit. The forces of outer space can transform even those things typically beneath our notice into vehicles for the decimation of everything with astonishing force and indifference. If our era is beginning to teach us anything, it is that here on earth, whatever objects we've dumped somewhere beyond us always come back to us, over and over again, and often with a vengeance. Timothy Morton describes our world as a hyperobject, one that forces us to rethink our old notions of what counts as the proper boundaries of things, or the borders between them:

> For some time we may have thought that the U-bend in the toilet was a convenient curvature of ontological space that took whatever we flush down it into a totally different dimension called *Away*, leaving things clean over here. Now we know better: instead of the mythical land Away, we know the waste goes to the Pacific Ocean or the wastewater treatment facility. Knowledge of the hyperobject Earth, and of the hyperobject biosphere, presents us with viscous surfaces from which nothing can be forcibly peeled. There is no Away on this surface, no here and no there.

If Timothy Morton's claim is that there is no "Away" to believe in any longer, because it has been revealed as an illusion, the wastes in space make that endless circularity especially vivid. In the very near future we won't need to leave the surface of the earth to know how true that is, or how consequential. The velocities that have sent our trash back to us with force and violence now seem to be coming down to earth too, as the consequences of global warming begin to register more and more vividly in everyday life, and our perceived smallness in the world and our corresponding smallness of impact suddenly return to us as part of collectively produced catastrophes. We are experiencing the terrors and fragilities of the minuscule made massive on earth, where in earlier times that nightmare only threatened to emerge from the terrible orbits in space.

4 MILLION-YEAR PANIC

There is a time signature and a haunted feeling to the desert that doesn't obtain anywhere else. In Sophie Fiennes' *The Pervert's Guide to Ideology*, the camera lingers longest on the emaciated carcasses of enormous airliners being slowly sunblasted into oblivion in the Mojave Desert, while in voiceover Slavoj Žižek proclaims the absolute necessity of seeing waste to understanding our contemporary crisis. The desert, as everyone knows, is where *they* bury things: the bodies of informants, NSA data collection centers, half-empty master-planned communities. Forcibly emptied of its native inhabitants in the nineteenth and twentieth centuries, the great southwestern deserts of the United States have since been filled with nuclear test sites and toxic waste dumps, while the steady erosion of living wages has seen the great American desert become yet another site of astonishing suburban encroachment, as people flee the coasts and city centers they can no longer afford or abide.

FIGURE 9

When our dams will have burst; when the sturdiest towers and fortresses and archives in our cities will have crumbled; when the languages we spoke and read will have been lost and our ancient books and thoughts will have been burned in the furnace of time; when the very notion of what counts as human will have been entirely rewritten or smudged out; when the shapes of the beaches and coastlines will appear almost unrecognizable; when the social and political and economic structures we treat as eternal will have been transformed into unrecognizable shapes; when all that we had ever thought and known and built will have receded into the deep mists of time; when all of this and more has passed, the great mountains of castoff sludge from our nuclear adventures will be the last of the last, their deadly isotopes decaying in the desert with the infinite patience of a bored immortal. Even a mere fifty thousand years hence— still millennia before our nuclear waste will have decayed— the firmament itself will have shifted as surely as the sands of all of the beaches of the earth will have been shifted by the pummeling tides. The Big Dipper, which forms part of the spine of the Great Bear, will be noticeably flatter, its handle bent. The Little Dipper will not look anything like a dipper anymore, its bottom edge now well above what used to be its top. The eye of Taurus will have fled from the rest of the bull's body, and Draco's serpentine form will have twisted and coiled and bent back in on itself. The club of Orion shall split; his shield shall burst apart like a blossoming flower. The stargazers of the far future will have to abandon the worn-out names we gave the heavens and replace them with true names.

When you are forced to contemplate what shapes the stars in the sky will someday take generations hence, you can no longer deny that waste has bested you. No human artifact ever conceived, and in all likelihood no human, whatever that will come to mean, will last even remotely as long as our nuclear waste. At such a remove from us, it no longer even makes sense to describe these undesirable objects as waste. For waste to be meaningful as a concept, we must be able to comprehend some manner of relationship between the waste object and its discarders, but in this instance that is no longer possible. We, and our inheritors, will have been laid waste, and everything else that had not been garbage. The radioactive hulk we had sequestered for an eternity will have traded places with us, as if, in a last derangement of the world we imagined ourselves to inhabit and possess, it had sloughed us off, rather than the reverse; as if we the wastemakers had become the waste product of time and the stubborn plutonium were the lord of all things. Our lives and bodies and thoughts, all the things we desired and the things we discarded, will appear as ghosts, as enigmatic bits

FIGURE 10

of drift in whatever minds or machines remain to pick us up from the long and crowded beach of history and wonder at what we were. Whatever else they will be, our nuclear waste, and the dim markers we will build to warn future civilizations away from it, will be a mausoleum, a requiem for the Anthropocene.

As John D'Agata, Sarah Zhang, and others have documented, the Waste Isolation Pilot Plant (WIPP) is a deep geologic repository in the Delaware basin of southeast New Mexico, not far from Carlsbad Caverns, where native people who lived in the area twelve to fourteen thousand years ago left behind pictographs and cooking rings that have already mostly vanished or been destroyed. Before they become more space debris, TRANSCOM satellites orbiting our planet monitor every movement of each shipment of our immense stockpiles of deadly transuranic wastes, all of which are unstable and decay radioactively. The waste is meant to be entombed deep beneath lakebeds, far below sea level in immense salt caverns. A vast land withdrawal act in 1992 enclosed some sixteen square miles of land from public use and all forms of entry. The optimistically named "Assurance Requirements," proposed for the building of facilities to house these wastes, cannot obscure the fact that there are many uncertainties involved in projecting even a few thousand years into the future, and they carry the whiff of fantasy, as do the elaborate array of "passive institutional controls" which were debated, discussed, and designed in an effort to construct reliable warning-system markers that would deter potential intruders and reduce the likelihood of inadvertent intrusion for the next few millennia. But as a nuclear waste consultant tells D'Agata in *About a Mountain*, "This waste is going to be deadly for tens of millions of years"—a statement that reminds you just how quaint the herculean efforts at WIPP are, and how terrifying.

Given these truly incomprehensible timelines, one does not have to read all 351 pages of the "Expert Judgment on Markers to Deter Inadvertent Human Intrusion into the Waste Isolation Pilot Plant" (but please do!) in order to understand just how impossible it will be to bury the radioactive waste securely and establish successful and enduring warning-system structures that could last many thousands of years. The goal is to use languages, star charts, images of facial expressions, elaborate symbols, earthworks, and more to—as its all-white, highly educated authors put it—"bypass the vagaries of cultural transformation." An almost entirely male set of experts registers this in passing as a particular challenge. Their proposals include an array of non-centered, uncomforting site designs a shunning of ideals, "irregular geometries and the denial of craftsmanship": Landscape of Thorns, Spike Field, Spikes Bursting Through Grid, Leaning Stone Spikes, Menacing Earthworks, Black Hole, Rubble Landscape, Forbidding Blocks. Will there be no more wandering fools centuries hence? If the future will exist, surely it will contain wandering fools. For my part, a rubble landscape or field of spikes sounds pretty amazing; it is easy to imagine future people (if they are anything at all like some of us) to be completely mesmerized and possessed by this architecture, drawn to it irresistibly. The last document in the immense WIPP dossier is a reply letter to its panelists from Carl Sagan. After thanking them for asking him to contribute his thoughts to the project of marking waste for untold centuries ("assuming the waste hasn't all leached out by then," he wryly adds), he proposes the skull and crossbones as the only conceivable symbol capable of having any hope of surviving the ages without mistranslation. Go ahead and include periodic charts, major languages, images of what the Big Dipper will look like, and more, he urges; but ultimately it's all about the skull and crossbones, our only hope of a sign to span the centuries.

As Sagan and a small number of the panelists recognized, the entire enterprise seems doomed to failure. Already, brine seepage in the salt beds could corrode the canisters; the contaminated water could find its way into the Rustler Aquifer, which feeds the Pecos River. An earthquake had already occurred in the region while the preliminary study was going on for the planned system. And there have already been leaks. On Valentine's Day 2014, a radiation leak occurred, its release area covering more than a mile and a half. The thirteen employees (none of whom were underground at the time of the leak) tested positive for internal radiological contamination. In light of some very basic problems evident practically from the outset of the project, the stated aim of bypassing the vagaries of cultural transformation and planning for millennia smacks of the same imperial hubris that underwrote a good deal of the activity that generated this nuclear waste in the first place: human domination of other humans. The long series of convoluted "Expert Judgments" read like nothing so much as a farce, a living document of our inability to comprehend even the most rudimentary things about the future: of technological de-evolution and a return to less technologically advanced technologies; the consequences of dramatic desertification and global climate catastrophes; the political, economic, social, and cultural transformations we cannot even begin to imagine; the question of which states might be in control, or if the things we call states will even persist in future ages; who or what our future generations will even be, in comparison to our own still mostly meatspace lives; or the darker question of whether or not people will survive at all. For this reason, what is most compelling about the entire apparatus constructed around the problem of nuclear waste is the bewildering *rhetorical* edifice constructed around it. The tone of these waste documents strives for authority, but everywhere is riddled with doubts, qualifiers, red flags, and minor terrors lurking in the footnotes. Every one of the monument ideas and containment ideas seems paltry, uninspired, ineffectual. The keep, the message kiosks, the berms and granite monoliths and time capsules, the empty edifices of human invention and construction and abandonment—it is a vision

FIGURE 11

of postmodernity's ruins that feels torn straight from the gray, windswept vistas of J. G. Ballard.

Discarding the idea to bury it in the permafrost (which, as it turns out, is rather impermanent), while believing that any meaningful solution to this human-made problem could be engineered, the WIPP dossier's immense archive of speculation and fancy speaks to what we might call a *selective futurity*. We are not solving the problem of automation or a post-work society, or the long unfolding crisis of global warming, or a hundred other things, but we profess to be committed to safeguarding our most devastating category of waste for eternity. This seems to be part of a larger relationship between humans and the wastes they produce. Our relationships to waste of all kinds, but especially this deadliest variety, always seem to depend on a fantasy of power, a belief that humankind shall have dominion over all things, including its own detritus; a steadfast faith in the idea that we will be the carriers of meaning, and not the invisible annihilation we have left in our wake. The WIPP and its marker project offer us the most profound example of the belief that our desires can annihilate, transcend, or master time and space. If a paint chip or a stray bolt can dismantle a spaceship, what buried container or grimacing face plate in the desert will even come close to doing its job? The WIPP speaks to the eternal dream of empire and the hubris of a vision for eternal hegemony; the desperate wish for technocratic and technological solutions to the confused muddle of history; the abiding faith in the stability of signs and architectural wonders; the obsession with security and boundaries and policing; and the poverty of imagination that allows cultures to create and employ weapons of annihilation without even possessing the skill to secure their leftovers.

As the organization Friends of the Pleistocene has argued, we have entered into a period in human history where we now create problems for which we cannot create solutions. And it seems increasingly clear that it will be our waste in particular that will serve as the record of the gap between them. Their series "Hedging on Stability" has been documenting the colossal efforts to contain radioactive waste at Fukushima after the meltdown of its nuclear reactors. "It seems to us," they say,

> that we've all just crossed a threshold, into a situation for which humans are now required to become massively creative and innovative at speeds, scales, and complexities that are without precedent—not, unfortunately, in the service of life-enhancing innovations and designs—but in the service of damage control and risk mitigation. Human lives and energies (as well as economies) will have to be redirected for untold futures in order to support this and other climate/environment altering endeavors.

Nuclear waste is our strongest material reminder that we have advanced to the stage in history where we create problems for which we cannot create solutions. Or, put differently, our solutions to specific problems inevitably generate newer and bigger problems. Some might argue that this is the human condition. If it is, then it is a condition we are endeavoring to foist on the posthuman ages as well. Unable to build a world where we do not deploy weapons of astonishing power and violence, we continue to believe we can build a world safe from the mountains of our deadly nuclear rubbish. This is where our investments in the future are directed: at mountains of undumpable waste, the great perilous remainder we have unleashed as a byproduct of our modern life. To consider nuclear waste and the WIPP is to consider a world in

FIGURE 12

which our garbage speaks in our stead, which is one way to imagine the failure of the project of humankind—as if to say: we have one message to give to the future, and that message is Death.

We live in a desperate world. Witness the carnivalesque atmosphere of the events surrounding the recent excavation of thousands of old unsold Atari *E.T.* video games from the New Mexico desert, where, the legends said, they had been quietly dumped decades before.

Just then a DeLorean pulled up in a cloud of dust. Out climbed Ernie Cline, author of *Ready Player One*, a novel about a future world improbably obsessed with the detritus of 1980s pop culture. From his DeLorean, outfitted with a mock flux capacitor, he pulled a Mattel Hoverboard and a flyer reading, "Save the Clock Tower!" Cline had arrived not from 1985 but from George R. R. Martin's house in Santa Fe; the *Game of Thrones* author had been borrowing the DeLorean for a private screening of *Back to the Future*. A noted connoisseur of 80s trivia, Cline was here to gush effusively for the cameras over any artifacts pulled from the ground. He wasted no time popping the trunk of his DeLorean and handing out copies of *Ready Player One*, inviting fans to a party he was hosting that evening at an arcade with go-karts and mini golf.

If adults of a certain age pine for lost childhood objects, the Atari dump site is what happens when middle-aged Gen X nostalgia, gamer culture, and the full corporate branding of everyday life have taken hold. For a certain broad class of people, Atari and *E.T.* are saturated with childhood memories. Manufacturers of video games in the 1980s had been dumping their excess game cartridges on the market at drastically reduced prices, but *E.T.* performed so poorly that the company was forced to take their overstock to the desert and bury it, and from that day until its unearthing in 2014, the legend grew.

The hype and elation surrounding the legend of the dumpsite and its recent excavation are partly explained by looking at the way that this particular waste site brings the form and content of 1980s nostalgia together. It neatly joins the legend's mysteries that swirled around its apocryphal details for years with the content of many of the pop culture touchstones of 1980s' American childhood. The primary obsession that drives the plots of *Goonies*, *Back to the Future*, *Raiders of the Lost Ark*, and so many other seminal 1980s films is the quest to excavate some talismanic relic of the past, or to recover, archaeologically, the mysteries and wonder buried in the suddenly recoverable past. The Atari dig, which on one level was simply about the pop cultural fascination with urban legends, delved much further into the terrain of its own time, place, and artifacts to generate a real-world manifestation of the kinds of stories on which 1980s childhood stories so often depended. The risks and rewards involved in an excavation of the past were the dominant motif of the major films of the time: the search for the Ark of the Covenant (*Raiders of the Lost Ark*), One-Eyed Willie's pirate treasure (*Goonies*), or the power to reshape the past itself (*Back to the Future*). As with *E.T.*, Steven Spielberg was a primary force behind all of these films. Like the canonical Atari console and the equally canonical *E.T.*, Spielberg shaped the popular consciousness of the 1980s, becoming, it is fair to say, the spirit animal of 1980s American childhood. Again and again his work returns to the sites of excavation and (re)discovery. Relentlessly he pines for a golden age of innocence, a return to youth and youthful possibilities, and the playfulness and simple joy that characterized his vision of that vanished past. The Atari dig is, in essence, a bad Spielberg film brought to life.

FIGURE 13

Piles of old discarded Atari games appeal to us because the objects of our childhood appeal to us—especially the *pop culture* objects of our childhood: comic books, cartoons, toys, cards, games. This form of nostalgia is not about recovering deep memories of earlier periods of life, or of reflecting on time's passage, but is part of a much larger cultural obsession (which Spielberg has perfected and exemplified) with resurrection of the lost totems of childhood and their capacity for a generational faux-solidarity. Because Atari, *E.T.* and the universes that Spielberg made are part of the lingua franca of those who came of age in the 1980s, this generational desire for collective identification through the Atari dig allows us to retreat into fantasies of shared culture. It is not just that it speaks to a generation's longing for the things of its collective childhood, but that our middle-aged capacity to keep pace with its increasingly sophisticated replacements or descendants in the millennial age has become increasingly impossible. Geekdom and pop culture literacy really began to become an art form and a way of thinking with the generation that came of age on video games and Spielberg films, and our constant need for nostalgia refresh and remix, our relentless engagement with the lifeworlds of gaming, cartoons, film, comics, and every other pop culture detritus that shaped so much of our self-conceptions, helps to explain why the Atari dig seemed so much more captivating than any number of other urban myths.

The desires that run beneath this type of nostalgia mark time through the steady succession of objects of affection, which, as we know, rarely last. Time sorts our beloved games and films and childhood memories into collections of objects that possess a talismanic or totemic power over us. The Atari dig reminds us that we have staked our nostalgia claims squarely in the pop culture debris of the time—the albums, movies, video games, and toys are for many of us inseparable from our sense of those decades; and pseudo-events like the Atari dig generate their significance and become memes or go viral in the present because this is where our collective memories have been centered. The common tongue of people old enough to engage in nostalgic trips with their friends—but still young enough to want to bother to do things like engage in nostalgic trips with their friends—is at least in part this glowing world of sugary childhood goodness. We adore all of these objects of the buried past, forgetting or being unbothered by the fact that in the process we were been trained to experience a specific kind of corporate-sponsored nostalgia, with its commodification of memory and its corporatization of the mind. The candy and soda, the TV shows, movies, and music; the toys; and now their offspring, the essential blogs and celebs and social media platforms; the new mobile tech; the apps, memes, and GIFs. As corporate life invades ever more corners of our everyday lives, so too will it come to pervade memory, desire, and character. Life, and reflection on one's life, becomes increasingly difficult outside of the spaces of corporate sanction and purview. Even if our relations to them are tangential or ironic or transgressive, they still serve this enlarging process. In this sense, the Atari dig has less in common with excavations than with the modern corporate product release. It keeps the hype machine, the crowds, the intrigue, the branding, but also folds in a pastness, not a futurity; the old, not the new. By standing in line to get the newest of the new iPhones we are not merely endeavoring to keep up with the cool things of the accelerating present, but trying to situate ourselves as participants in what now passes for an event, a stage-managed consumption cycle that we can already feel being pulled into the past.

5 RUINISM

We should resist the temptation to see waste only where trash-objects themselves are visible. Every place is a place of waste; it's just unevenly distributed in space and time. It is not just that some of us are in the melancholy or perverse habit of looking upon new and unbroken things and seeing in them their future status as rubbish; it is that these places and things are already repositories of waste in many forms. They just shield it from view, when we look at them with an eye toward a narrower concept of what counts as waste in our minds. Just as our memories have been built in the houses of corporate patronage, we've been trained to look for waste in the dumpster, the gutter, washing ashore; in the branches, or sequestered deep underground. Those are the classes of things we are taught to call waste. But there are also counterintuitive and obscured "sites" of waste. At some point of attention, waste can't be *only* an assemblage of detritus; it's also the trashscapes we call Fifth Avenue, the malls, the glossy polished retailers. For my part, the truly unsettling landscape of trash isn't the one at the dump or in the gutter, but the "clean" home that is taken to be our ideal, and which is reified in every film, TV show, and advertisement as embodying the proper relationship of humankind to the veritable mountains of waste we produce. The clean surfaces that contemporary consumer society presents to us as the ideal should trouble us at least as much as the stereotypical pile of smelly trash or filthy hovel does. That they so seldom do is an indication of just how pervasively consumer culture has enmeshed its aesthetic into ancient notions of cleanliness and pollution. It is all built on a vision of cleanliness and happiness that cannot last.

FIGURE 14

In one scene in *The Black Power Mixtape 1968–1975*, we see a busload of people on what has come to be known as a "ghetto tour," where curious and slightly daring travelers gawk at the unkempt fringes of cities. The idea of the ghetto tour gerrymanders thoughts about waste, situating it squarely within the squalor or privation evident in the regions of town where the working poor or the indigent must of necessity gather in order to survive. This is not, I would argue, all that different from the phenomenon of "toxic tourism," an ostensibly progressive notion that brings people into devastated communities on "toxic tours." Phaedra Pezzullo describes tours of toxic sites as a kind of negative sightseeing, a method for cultivating environmental advocacy. Also known as "disaster tourism," these are well-intentioned efforts to make vivid for outsiders the wastage of other places. But disaster tourism and "ghetto" tourism, for all of their affective differences, are two sides of the same coin. In one, we are meant to survey the damage wrought by the very unromantic forms of waste that actually destroy lives on a daily basis through the slow violence of unemployment, poverty, overpolicing, and gentrification, while on the other, we are meant to engage in a bit of armchair anthropology as we tour, rather briskly, the human wastespaces of capital, the repulsive alternative spaces that are meant to contrast with the major attractions of the given metropolis. Toxic tourism might seem somewhat less odious, since we would like to think that people signing up to go look at Superfund sites or cancer alleys or petrochemical wastescapes understand something about desiccated zones that tourists zipping quickly through the ghetto might not. And yet in terms of the particular kind of spatial relationship each provides, they are functionally equivalent. We are either meant to see the gritty and authentic underbelly of the American metropolis as we breeze through its seedier parts on safari, or we are meant to contemplate the horrible spectacle of smokestacks, bilge ponds next to playgrounds, and waste dumps to goad us into action. In either case, we are still comfortably ensconced in some role as outsider to them; otherwise the tour part makes no sense. And it is this shared reliance on voyeurism, spectacle, and perceived difference that joins these otherwise distinct phenomena and demands further reflection. Reading these trashscapes in this way is easier to do when one is at a comfortable distance from the stories of penury and misery they tell. If political economy always ends up showing its face in spatial relations, the rotting hearts of industrial brownswards must be experienced by the viewer or visitor as at least partially and alien. He must see himself as gazing upon something he is not himself fully engulfed in; otherwise the aesthetic fascination of these vistas, whether for prurient interest or out of liberal sympathies, is lost. Poverty and want are concepts born out of structures of oppression; *place* is merely where some of their features are made easily visible to outsiders.

Nowadays we call this Detroitism, or, more often, ruin porn: the haunting allure of those proliferating image banks of rotted cities, hollowed-out industrial centers, abandoned byways, and relics of a preglobalized economy. "Ruin porn" is a terrible phrase, but an informative one, in its way. You know we're at a very specific moment in globalization when every outlet feels compelled to offer its own disquisition on the phenomenon. A quick and very partial tally would include *WIRED* (which even has the term as a discrete search category), *Medium*, *Guernica*, *The Daily Beast*, *PopMatters*, *Utne Reader*, *The Wilson Quarterly*, *The Atlantic*, *Nautilus*, and many more. The phrase took hold as a descriptor for a number of reasons. If pornography is on one level about the construction of stable, homogenizing forms of displaying and generating pleasure and desire, it's more meaningfully dependent on an unmuddied voyeurism. To work as fantasy, pornography must depend on the viewer's distinct absence and distance, or clear sense of separation, from the scene. He must see himself as looking at something in which he takes no actual part, and any technologies that enable this (film, photography, the internet) achieve their titillating results partly by virtue of the voyeur's sense of himself as an outsider looking in. Scrubbed of the sexual elements, this same logic is operative in "ruin porn" too, where the aesthetic pleasure or horror or curiosity depends largely on the ability of the viewer to disentangle himself from the ruination he is seeing in front of him. As with other forms of voyeurism, ruin porn reveals something important about our emerging relationships to the new post industrial wastelands we have created and then left to rot: like all the other forms, it also traffics in a reliable repetition of subjects, tropes, and motifs, and offers a fundamentally conservative register of engagement with its putative object of decay. Like other voyeuristic indulgences, it offers one of the easiest paths to manufactured desire (now, the desire to see oneself as having been spared the fate of these collapsed ruins), and the emptiest.

Romantic adoration of ruins in the Diderotian mode is only possible where the belief in a present and a correspondingly connected future still persists, and where the benefits of a certain level of social and economic privilege allow these musings to exist within a space safe from the true depredations of waste that others must suffer in other circumstances. No one actually living through the decimation and end of all things, no one dying from pollution or surviving in a community choked with filth, would look upon the decay of the world and find beauty in it; but a sufficiently comfortable subject-citizen, on tour among the necropolises of old, indulging in a daytrip into the remnants of the past, can allow himself to find something majestic and noble in the demise of peoples and communities and civilizations that are not his. In this sense, "ruin porn" repeats that Romantic vantage point, but with a rusty, post-industrial twist. This posture allows you to look upon the thing that you believe to be closer to death than you seem to be, and is therefore available for all sorts of high-minded romantic notions of beauty, time, and other such things. It is not that contemplation of the ruins, in provoking thoughts of the decline of our own empires, lives, and dreams, somehow compels us to withdraw into ourselves and seek new measures, to behave differently. These romantic thoughts flicker, then sputter out; and what we are left with is our own continuing breath, our own confident stride in our stirring city. Far from forcing a complete reevaluation of our own lifeworld, contemplation of the ruins is easily bracketed from everything fresh and new outside of it. The ruin casts its shadow, and we return to the light of the present, vaguely wiser, perhaps, but no less committed to propping up our own decaying edifices, for most of us can see no other way forward from there. It must recede from our consciousness, as we have learned to let so much else recede: the waste we casually pile up out of sight, the nightmares of history that pave the paths we walk, the reality-denial that allows us to soldier on blindly in the face of facts and realities that threaten to undermine and engulf everything.

Our contemporary fascination with wastescapes is related to a much larger problem of spectacle and visibility, and the political, social, economic, moral, and environmental consequences of our growing reliance on them. Why are contemporary accounts of waste inexorably drawn to capturing it through image and spectacle? Knowledge and language seem important, but incomplete (as when we say, "Pics or it didn't happen"). And why does waste need to be visible to us as a dangerous object for us to think about waste, and to act? As Max Liboiron at the *Discard Studies* blog notes, 97 percent of waste is not the municipal solid waste that all of us create and are familiar with, but *industrial* waste. Liboiron is right to note that a responsible chronicle of the truly meaningful and consequential landscapes of waste would not consist of landfills and garbage cans but of things like oil sands, mines, and decapitated mountains—all of the extractive industrial processes that are ravaging the planet.

A society of constantly accelerating production, even in the face of recurring periods of economic crisis and collapse, must do more than continually stimulate consumer desire and expand its credit economies. It must also continually endeavor to obscure the specific nature of its production processes (resource extraction, labor, organization); and it must also do what it can to mitigate or suppress the reality

FIGURE 15

and impacts of its various waste products. If the mass of consumers truly beheld the gruesome nature of production and effluent on either side of the sites of consumption and use/enjoyment, the entire system would collapse. We do not often see or smell or taste the garbage in our air, our soil, our water, and so we keep breathing and drinking, just as we do not see our cargo ships and cars and planes and air-conditioning units *directly* annihilate the coastline, or eradicate species, or give us cancer. It's even less common to see firsthand the kind of wastelands that Liboiron describes, for the same reason that it's so rare for us to see the inner workings of an industrial slaughterhouse or the grim buildings where our phones are made.

In the face of the image, language seems like a poor advocate for thinking waste. The image is time-bound. Every photographic image is an artifact at least indirectly obsessed with time, and our natural predisposition toward spectacle, our privileging of the looking eye over the reading eye, draws our gaze instantly to even the tiniest bits of waste. In fact it often seems as if waste and photography were made for each other. It is impossible not to see the coffee cup, the soggy paper, the plastic bird, the cigarette butt, the piles of busted furniture. Our films are littered with litter; our galleries are heaped up with photos and sculptures; and stagings are overrun with trash. But even so, there are good reasons to be sick of the society of the spectacle. It made a certain amount of sense in the previous century, when photography was new and industry, for all its size, was nowhere near as immense as it is now. We should consider the possibility that our longstanding tradition of privileging the image may have outlived some of its usefulness. If we consider that nearly all of what we would call waste is being churned up in places that are well guarded and closed to the public, powerful images might not be the smartest thing to be looking for. We can already see the poverty of imagery most forcefully in the ongoing calls to bear witness to climate catastrophe: calving glaciers, drowning polar bears. The decimation of the environment proceeds at a staggering pace and scale, but is generally only registered by onlookers who can gaze upon visual evidence of its impact—and that is actually a huge part of the problem.

In the meantime, Ed Burtynsky's seminal photographic work seems to play on this desire to bear witness to human impacts on the environment. The visual register of Burtynsky's large-scale photographs of industrial-scale production, mining, energy capture, and waste disposal sites may induce all kinds of emotions in the viewer, but certainly awe would be among them, even if it exists alongside horror, disgust, or sorrow. Their subjects may be on modern industrial practices but the form speaks to something else, almost reverential, in its execution. The aesthetic care and beauty in Burtynsky's images—the distance and vantage points, but also the color saturation, the unrelenting immensities on which his camera lingers, along with the immense scales of his work—can just as easily have the opposite effect that one might expect good-hearted environmentally minded viewers to adopt.

Before these tableaux we are all helpless and infinitesimal in the face of what our own societies are doing to the only planet we have. In *Burtynsky: Water*, the photos of phosphor tailings ponds in Florida are glorious and gorgeous, as if we were seeing into the pulsating mind of the planet itself, its frenzied ganglia swimming in cerulean fire. So too are the images taken of Bombay Beach, a sewage treatment plant in the California desert. From Burtynsky's vantage point, the enormous pools of sewage look like nothing less than a gigantic Technicolor paintbox. In *Burtynsky: Oil*, he devotes significant space to the petroleum industry of Kern County. We see the vast pumpjack fields of Taft, the ground and sky suffused with a dingy brown funk, the Sierra Nevada mountains dimly visible through the haze of carcinogenic smog. Whether taking photos of the Alberta oil sands, the SOCAR extraction fields in Azerbaijan, giant scrapyards of U.S. Air Force bombers, fighters, and dead helicopters at AMARC in Tucson, the vistas of ferrous bushling in Canada (which looks like the most ornate and airy abstract art piece imaginable, a mass of microscopic astonishment), densified oil drums, or tire piles, the sense one gets in peering through all this immense grime is one of a frenzied activity, a dirty vitality. In Alex MacLean's photography, in Stephen Hirsch's *Gowanus: Off the Water's Surface* (a collection of disturbingly pretty photos of New York City's most polluted and disgusting body of water), as well as in the works of many others, we discover this aesthetic of the glorious saturated imagery of wastescapes. Together they constitute something like a production sublime, as toxic, high-volume, post-production, and post-consumer waste is repackaged and framed at a scale and in a manner that minimizes waste's catastrophic causes and effects and foregrounds the things in it that are beautiful instead.

This type of waste photography shows us that anything can look like something else or be made to look beautiful, provided you're looking from a certain vantage point. In commenting on his own work Burtynsky has often emphasized the relatively agnostic (or at least undidactic) approach he means to take in terms of the image. These images seem cleansed of the contemplations of waste that Bataille found so disconcerting, the fetid, putrid elements of organic decay we see, that invariably push us toward revulsion. Even in the rare "dirty" pictures of waste here, there is something off about them, something not just orderly but proud of that orderliness. In his photos of oil recycling and shipbreaking in Bangladesh (one of the few scenes in his work where individual human beings actually occupy a large or central place, wearing coats of crude oil like second skin), there is something unnervingly demure, even stately, about their composition. The disgust and despair of a life that begins and ends among the wastescapes of the globalized world is missing. This is not because Burtynsky does not care about the plight of wasted humanity and wasted planets, but it does suggest that if you want to try to document the true scale of globalization, you may very well sacrifice a certain intimacy, personalization, and pain. Spectacles of waste in the ruin porn mode, or the production sublime mode, confront us with the possibility that the best thing of all we could do with waste is to change course, and to try to think our way through it without ogling it at all.

6 SPLINTER, SHARD, AND STONE

In *On the Natural History of Destruction*, W. G. Sebald's account of the ruination of German cities during the Second World War, we are told that the scale of the new wastelands that had once been Hamburg and other thriving cities is so overwhelming and so alien to everyday conceptions of life that the survivors staggering aimlessly through the wreckage are not only unable to speak of the devastation, but also, in many instances, literally unable to see it, to look upon it, and face it squarely, as a rational outsider might at least attempt to do. In shock, they wander half-dead through the wreckage as if the city had always looked exactly like this.

This is the terrain of the waste we call rubble. The vantage point from which Burtynsky had staged his images gave a sense of orderliness to the immensity of the blasted wastescapes he documented. If it was not always a bird's-eye view, exactly, it still retained something of the stately and serene view available from a great and slightly dispassionate distance. But in the case of rubble, the object's original and desirable state is no longer visible; its pieces cannot be glued together or reassembled. It has been ground down, pulverized. Existing somewhere after beauty, and mostly even beyond salvage, rubble offers only a scrap heap where once a cathedral stood. These are not the pleasurable ancient remnants that Rose Macaulay described, because they are more accurately understood, at least from our own selfish vantage point, as *premature ruins*: the rapid decimation of the places and object-worlds that had been, moments before, the places where people lived, worked, and loved. They are too close to our passage through them to be available for romantic thoughts of vanished splendor; they are reluctantly admitted to the archive of waste by virtue of their sudden

FIGURE 16

and unexpected devastation. These are the things that have been laid waste, and in the process they mark, as the plastic innards of Jordan's birds had, a defamiliarizing stage in our relationship to the things we desire and the things we discard. It marks the transition from discrete objects to mere material, a return to rawness. Rubble is another name for interrupted desire.

Now it is not just traditional wars like those described by Sebald that produce mountains of rubble, but the entire class of things we might call *climate debris*: matter out of place, born from the hurricanes, floods, tsunami, and wildfire disasters—the Sandys, Katrinas, and Fukushimas—that we had hoped our object-worlds were built to withstand. Its imagery brings to mind the jigsaw puzzle, loads of kindling, enormous piled matchsticks. It is that special class of obliterated objects you see in aerial flyover shots after a hurricane or flood or tornado, the wreckage that political leaders walk through briskly before they offer speeches about fortitude and resilience. What separates climate debris from garden-variety heaps of rubbish is the temporal short-circuit of our causal relationship to it. The allure of this particular kind of waste is intense. Any film involving a natural or manmade catastrophe cannot help itself: it must survey the wreckage; it must show the astonished, numbed, horrified, rattled countenances of the straggling survivors. It must dwell on its accumulated immensity; its pulverized miniatures arrayed in gigantic edifices to the power of annihilation.

The debris field is the preeminent object of visual grandeur in our contemporary age of crisis. We have reached an age of the miniaturization of technologies and the virtualization of experience. When combined with the erasure of scenes of traditional industry from everyday life and the abandonment of projects of immense public works of monumentality or infrastructure, debris fields produce in us a rare and readymade fascination with scenes of monumental climate waste. We approach the individual and collective artifacts of our instant wastelands with shock and incomprehension, and are summoned to the realization that, as Timothy Morton says, "we humans are playing catch-up with reality." The fact is that when we look at climate debris fields and piles of rubble, wherever and however we look at it—on the train tracks, tangled in the branches, or towering over us in great stinking smoking piles—we comprehend almost nothing. Our thoughts about waste are often formed on the basis of a certain unwarranted faith in the proper lifespan of particular objects (cars, homes, cities). We had been living in expectation that time would unfold in a certain way, relatively peaceful and calm, and then these sudden mountains of ruin remind us that these expectations had been based on the lie we tell ourselves: that we are time's master, when it was always the opposite that was true. Climate debris interrupts and mangles; it hands back to us the broken fragments of the wholes we had made, and we stand before it dumbfounded.

Barely visible in the far background of Burtynsky's images of Kern County oil fields, the small isolated town in the Sierra

Nevada mountains where I grew up was a landscape of empty storefronts, tumbleweeds piled against wind-toppled fences, lone sun-scorched men shuffling destinationless down the thin edge of the roadside, collapsed barns, unwheeled jalopies propped on blocks in weed-choked yards, busted farm equipment left to rust in the sun. It was, and remains, the place I know more intimately than any other. A place that, like Robert Smithson's Passaic, contained no true ruins, but only the wreckage of possible futures that had been abandoned: of exterminated natives, drought-wrecked ranches and hungry cattle, gold strikes that came to naught, recreation towns falling into crumbling dams, drying lakes, and the dust that comes with disuse.

Each summer, before the woods and scrublands of the west dried out and the great fires tore their way reliably across the hills, we would venture up the plateau to harvest our winter's supply of firewood. While the adults felled trees and cut timber, I would hunt for flakes of obsidian cast off by populations that had been native to these mountain ranges centuries before the arrival of the prospectors, ranchers, settlers, retirees, and the U.S. Army. The term that archaeologists use to denote the waste flakes generated in the long and sophisticated production of stone tools is *debitage*. I'd most often find them on the edges of masses of exposed granite that earlier people had used as worksites. I would dig through the understory surrounding the rocks and gather these fragments in empty plastic film containers and surreptitiously bring them home, since the adults would not have tolerated my acts of desecration, if they'd known about them. These tiny flecks of glassy brown-black stone were probably the first things I ever stole. I coveted them in a way I have never coveted anything since, in part because of the secretive nature of their procurement and the thrilling challenge of finding them, but most of all because, like some ravenous nineteenth-century Egyptologist, I desperately coveted any objects that had been touched by ancient hands. And unlike the glass-encased curios of antiquity to be found in every museum, this detritus was out there in the dirt, a stone's throw from home, waiting to be found; a proximity which I felt gave me license to run roughshod over it, taking what I wanted and discarding the rest.

While the native populations pushed out by the WIPP in the southwestern desert were predominantly Navajo, further west in the lower Sierra Nevada range it was mostly Tubatulabal, Foothill Yokuts, Paiute, and Monache. William Hildebrant and Kelly McGuire tell us that there was a fluorescence of obsidian biface production industry in this region in the Middle Archaic period. In subsequent years, when gold prospectors, soldiers, and ranchers began to make their way into the region in the mid-nineteenth century, these lithic tools and debris would become the most common elements of the local archaeological record. The bedrock mortars in these areas are relatively deep, smooth-bored depressions in the bedrock where native peoples would grind acorns, pine nuts, manzanita berries, and small game. Cut with immense craft and precision, and a great deal of labor, these mortars would eventually begin to fill up with rainwater, pine needles, twigs, leaves, and duff, sometimes completely obscured under a carpet of needles and leaves that extended across the entire bedrock, so that if you were to have walked past the rocks, or even to have walked atop them, surveying the area, you might not even have seen that they were there until you got down on hands and knees and

FIGURE 17

swept the detritus of the forest away to reveal them, as usable and impermeable now as they were centuries hence.

These spaces are generally referred to as "midden," and they usually aligned with activity areas involved in acorn and other food processing in the Sierra Nevada range. As Thomas Jackson argues, these food-processing sites "represent the creation by women of *fixed production facilities* on the landscape which are related directly to the organization of women's labor and production." The midden soils had a high density of artifacts and other occupational debris, among them arrowhead shards, pestles, and handstones. As Terry Jones notes, obsidian was one of the most important trade items in the central and southern Sierra in the pre-settler period. In the complicated topography of these lands, river canyons on one side of the high ragged mountains descended to shallow high-altitude valleys and the immense San Joaquin basin, while the mountainous terrain on the eastern side of the range led directly into the enormous and grueling deserts of the American Southwest. Unlike the sharp and glassy obsidian, the stony local granite most prevalent across these regions was relatively unsuitable for fine stone tools. The wide range of game across the area (deer, antelope, black bear, bobcat, mountain lion, squirrel, rabbit), along with the unreliability of inland creeks and natural fisheries, meant that hunting would form an important supplement to the foraging that often sustained the native peoples struggling to survive in challenging conditions. For this reason, the use of obsidian in arrowhead, spear-tip, and skinning-knife production would have been incredibly important and common across the Sierras as a whole. As the research presented in the essays in Joan Gero's collection *Engendering Archaeology: Women and Prehistory* notes, "Prehistoric women are probably disproportionately represented in densely concentrated areas of household refuse, and archaeological materials from the central areas of base-camp or house-floor excavations are at least *likely* to be associated with women's work." Gero refers to these labor spaces, where only small handfuls of wastestone persist, as the terrain of *genderlithics*. Her work is among the most important contributions to the dismantling of the specious longstanding argument that stone tool manufacture was an exclusively or predominantly male activity. Most of the obsidian flakes I'd find were buried at the base of bedrock mortar outcroppings, where many years before they had been sheared from the main arrowheads or bifaces being sculpted by women sitting atop the rocks and sent tumbling down to land at the base among the chunks of bark, cones, and pine needles that blanketed the soil, leaving behind a debris field much like the pattern of chopped hair you find upon getting up from the barber's chair you'd been seated in. Thinking of the labor these women performed to produce the weapons and implements necessary for survival called to mind the thin brown and orange slivers of potato and carrot that would fill our kitchen sink when my mother was peeling vegetables for a stew.

Like countless other trespassers before and since, I would find these vestiges of old sites where homes were made and bring them to my home, where I would arrange and display them on a shelf near my bed. At some later point, they were cast off again, probably tossed into the trash bin one day alongside food scraps and plastic packaging, on a day when these beautiful shards suddenly meant much less to me than they once had. And now they are sequestered somewhere beneath the compacted earth of the Kern Valley dumpsite, where they will likely remain until some future archaeologist or rubbish-seeker unearths them once more, nestled amongst our heaps of plastic twentieth-century trash. In their smallness, those shards had no value as arrowheads or tools for skinning or cutting, but as objects shaped by human hands many years before, this glassy debris meant everything to me, as something you've cast off yesterday might be of interest to a bored child many years hence. These chunks and flecks of obsidian are like the sawdust, shavings, and weld droplets of their time: the signs of manufacture of the tools of basic survival, left behind as the inevitable waste castings, but appearing to my young eyes, and others like me, as wondrous shards of an unrecoverable past. A glassy black from a distance, up close most of these thin shards shone with a deep brown color. When I would find ones that were large and thin enough, I would bring them home and run them across the printed words in books I was reading. For some reason I found reading under brown glass quietly thrilling, as if I had stumbled upon magical spectacles that would grant me access to the words beneath the words, the true meanings of language that I always found myself dwelling in whenever I wasn't outdoors harvesting stonewaste from ages past.

But the most striking thing about these particular shards was that the labor that went into creating the gorgeously stippled and crenellated surfaces of these sophisticated obsidian tools and weapons was visible in the objects themselves. They gave off an intimation of work and worry that so many of the other objects we now hold have been designed to minimize or erase, so that our smooth gleaming phones and other devices appear to at least some of us almost ethereal, the labor embodied in them almost invisible to those who do not know where to see it. As the glittering waste products of home economies from years past, this debitage, like the glass jars at Dead Horse, seemed to whisper something about the laborious past that is always hidden just beneath the surface of things in our frenetic present. More so than anything I ever read in books, those small glassy discoveries in the dirt spurred my young curiosity about the past and its obscured histories, and all the ways that our labor, like so much about else about us, is always being erased.

7 WHERE THE HOARD IS

Desire is idiosyncratic and individual, and this is especially the case where it lowers its threshold for satisfaction and finds its outlet in objects. For rich and poor alike, our assembled things matter in ways that are nontransferable and mostly untranslatable to others; I can loathe or tolerate or be respectful of or indifferent toward your things, and you toward mine, but we will never be in perfect accord. And it is sometimes difficult to know which objects to hold on to as time passes. Tastes and interests change; living arrangements, partners, families, income, spaces, and priorities change. We clutch certain mementos and wake up one day wondering where and why we ever let go of others which now suddenly seem so important to us. Our objects are supposed to say something about who we are—or who we've been or would like to be. They drag their subjective and charged histories with them. In "Marx's Coat," Peter Stallybrass describes the Marx family's (and by extension the entire working classes') complicated attachment of value to the small hoard of objects they held so precariously from the pawnbrokers. The sentimental and familial values all had to be routinely cleansed from these objects by the broker and the family so that they could re-enter the marketplace unencumbered, as mere commodities. "What little wealth they had was stored not as *money* in *banks*," he notes, "but as *things* in the *house*. Well-being could be measured by the comings and goings of those things." The back and forth of these objects' relation to competing forms of use and value was its own kind of endless litigation: the way that the chipped saucers and soiled fustian of daily hardscrabble existence were constantly having to be wrenched from home and released back into the market, if only to be desperately bought back again for a spell. In telling their endless saga of penury, the movements of Marx's clothes away from home and back again also tell the story of the way desire clings to objects. What an object is worth—which is to say whether or not it is garbage yet—is a function of the individual's taste, but also the market's needs at the same time; and a large part of the experience of poverty is seeing just how radically opposed those desires often are.

Death is another reminder of these shifting values. One of the many unpleasant but inevitable conversations that take place when a loved one is dying or has recently died concerns the future disposition of their life's accumulated objects. One of the things that is most alienating about visiting another person's home is surveying the odd object choices they've made: what they hang on their walls, the rug pattern they seem so fond of, the curios and tchotchkes, the engine blocks or cowprint curtains they've chosen to surround themselves with. As Mary Douglas warned us, "There is no such thing as absolute dirt. It exists in the eye of the beholder." Venture into a certain type of yard sale and you will discover the coats, belts, purses, ties, armchairs, chiffarobes, dinette sets, and appliances of other tastes and other times. With the passing of these people their objects are released anew into a world that they have often been kept shut out of for many years, and the light of the present cannot help but reveal the dust and age and tackiness of the recent or distant pasts that those objects bear as traces within them. If life in a modern consumer society involves the accumulation of objects (picture frames, 8-tracks, cookie jars, cheese graters, handmade quilts, lone mittens), death expels them into a new and untethered life, where new and harsh scales of value are laid upon them and judgments rendered in a swift and merciless order. Sometimes waste is taste, and nothing more.

Look around the homes of loved ones whose objects you might at some future date have the opportunity to inherit or be saddled with sorting through, and lament how few of them have a meaning for you that is anywhere nearly as profound as they do for this person who means everything to you. And then return home, to your own piles of things, and see if you are able to see within them their own future obsolescence: not just as objects that will fall out of use, or into disrepair, or out of style, but out of favor with whatever child or heir or rummaging stranger will inevitably come to them once you are gone. Of the things that mattered to you somehow, almost none will mean anything for them. The object-world we build around ourselves is as fragile and artificially maintained as we are, and just as prone to dissolution. For the most part, the world beyond you will not care about your furniture, your kitchen utensils, your musty clothes, your tchotchkes, or your precious books. The only thing that holds a collection of things together is the person who had gathered and held them across the long years of her life, and considered them an integral part of herself; and now she is gone.

American Pickers, a staple of the History Channel lineup of faux-reality shows, follows the cross-country peregrinations of Mike and Frank, two junk collectors ("pickers") from Iowa who roam the back roads of rural America in search of "rusty gold," the detritus of earlier times buried under piles of rubble, squirreled away in attics and sagging barns. Their primary business is rediscovering and then selling things they've found in the nooks and crannies of the American heartland to collectors, designers, and homeowners in more affluent parts of the country. The majority of the show consists of them tunneling through immense piles of stuff that individual hoarder-collectors have accumulated over the past forty or fifty years and are now ready to sell.

Mike goes out of his way to talk about finding a new and proper home for these derelict objects by returning them to market. While his enthusiasm seems genuine—he has the simple rugged charm of a knowledgeable and self-deprecating Midwesterner—the premise of the show and the survival of their business depends on locating people with immense piles of old junk who are ready to sell at substantial discounts, as well as a pool of largely-unseen buyers eager to pay handsomely for these pieces of vintage Americana. Mike and Frank, along with their small coterie of co-workers, assistants, siblings, and associates, thus serve a critical transactional function for the ongoing process of looting the object-worlds of America's past to produce new commodities built on our modern desires for objects of the past that have managed to survive and captivate us with their now-exotic craftsmanship. Mike will often speak of his desire to bring the junked object back "into the world" by giving it a new life. The Indiana octogenarian's obsession and frugality become the mechanism by which overpriced Brooklyn or Silicon Valley micro-lofts are decorated in "signature pieces" meant to signify some kind of imagined relation to the past, authenticity, craft, and labor flensed of everything except the aestheticized totem-object that is supposed to embody them.

In his work on the theory of objects, Jean Baudrillard asked what lies behind "the persistent search for old things— for antique furniture, authenticity, period style, rusticity, craftsmanship, hand-made products, native pottery, folklore, and so on?" As he argues, "The tense of the mythological object is the perfect: it is that which occurs in the present as having occurred in a former time, hence that which is founded upon itself, that which is 'authentic.'" There is an

FIGURE 18

entire lost world of manual production that these objects, in their rugged beauty and durability, communicate to us; and it echoes in the vanishing world of the junkmen themselves, who have served as unofficial curators of the bygone days of American craftsmanship. But beyond all of this there is the somewhat newer world of antique-sprinkled homes and businesses, seeking to present the aura of "history" detached from actual material lives, reduced now to mere curios. These new business and home spaces now serve as the museum and mausoleum of material worlds of capital production that have migrated elsewhere.

In *American Pickers*, this desire for the imaginary authenticity emanating from old rusted objects also functions as an old-guard nativism in disguise. The patrons are in most cases elderly white men living in rural backwaters of America. Not coincidentally, this mirrors the show's and the channel's target demographics. In this sense, the show not only uncovers "History" by way of dusting off the derelict objects and equipment of an earlier age of American manufacture, but also offers viewers a palliative for the aggrieved status of these junkmen who seem to have outlived their time or usefulness, as being worn-out relics themselves. These living fossils from the American Century serve as jovial, wizened spokesmen for the vanished worlds of the Second World War era and midcentury lifeways. Over and over again they make their case for returning affection and attention (and a tidy profit) to dismal objects that once appeared to have outlived their usefulness. These guardians of the past have, it seems, staved off the complete annihilation of these cast-iron banks, gas-station pumps, folk art, and decaying motorcycle engines for just a little while longer. But *American Pickers* is more than just a primer in white American nostalgia-panic at the perceived loss of Arcadian industrial-era America. There's also a clear generational politics at work in the show, although it's always presented in a rather romanticized, diffuse way: there was a time, the show laments, when this country used to build things.

Lamentably, the show is one of the few on contemporary television to give any airtime to senior citizens. We're meant to see the collectors themselves, and not merely their piles of junk, as relics of a bygone time—of a present that no longer has the space, patience, or interest in the detritus of an earlier time, whether the cast-off objects of those eras or the people who lived most of their lives in them. By being attuned to the demise of the age of American manufacture and its attendant phenomena—the erosion of class mobility, job security, and community—through a neck-deep ramble among the rust and antiques, the show serves as a living document of the many shapes that wastelands take in the age of globalization. The mini-biographies given of the collectors on the show also offer us a striking, if fleeting, glimpse into the quiet lives of the Second World War and Vietnam generations in the early decades of the new century. These generations used to be at cross-purposes a few decades ago, but within the purview of the show they have coalesced into a vast Retirementland, where the distinctions between the Second World War Korean War, and Vietnam War veterans are effectively meaningless. For students of American political history, there is a strange flattening effect in seeing the differences between sixty-year-old Vietnam vets and eighty-five-year-old Second World War vets being effectively erased. The generational conflict of the New Left era, with its deep suspicions of and disengagement from the culture and values of the generation that preceded it, collapses in *American Pickers* into a new formulation of a broader industrial American past, one in which there are those who came of age in America before the great neoliberal transformations of the 1970s and beyond, and those of us who came after. These are men who worked a forty-year job and bought a home and some land and started a family, accumulating a lifetime of junk in the process that they now display with avuncular pride. What the culture wars of midcentury did, globalization neatly undoes, now uniting a broader swath of "authentic" American experience by unsettling the old political divides that no longer obtain and replacing them with a new type of division, between the age of good old-fashioned grit and industry, and the new fallen age of store-bought faux-authenticity.

The show makes a fascinating and antagonistic counterpoint to the TV show *Hoarders* and its even more sensationalist TLC variation *Hoarding: Buried Alive*, both of which milk the hoarder's collection-compulsion for every ounce of pathos it's worth. To a far greater degree than *American Pickers*, *Hoarders* depends for its pathos on the lingering, voyeuristic spectacle of unseemly and unhealthy rubbish. Where *American Pickers* offers a folk archaeology, *Hoarders* provides us with the worst kind of pop psychology. It appeals to our perverse fascination with social deviations, mania, obsessions, the landscapes of psychological disorders or defects. The shows offer competing portraits of people's relationship to the objects of their affection, suggesting that objects (even in great quantities) are neither good nor bad; only one's relationship to them is. The producers of these shows frame their respective junk-heaps in markedly different ways: the piles in *Hoarders* are always filled with spoiled food, rotting papers, dead animals; in *American*

Pickers they contain cast-iron toys and rare nineteenth-century bicycles. But even a cursory glance at the immense piles of objects the pickers find in even the richest seam of antiques makes clear that the vast majority of material owned by the people in *American Pickers* is also certifiably worthless rubbish. The question this leaves unasked or unanswered: Might the depraved hoarders have some items of genuine material or historical value buried among the wreckage of old leftovers, dirty dishes, and mouse turds? Occasionally, we are given glimpses of this, but it's quickly elided, since the objective of the show is completely different. Here all that we survey is waste, and nothing more.

Placed side by side, these two shows about waste and desire also indicate that what counts as value depends on what the market wants and what social norms dictate as being something deserving of individual desire. The market and the social conventions of reality TV are thus the proper judge of character. If your home is filled with moldy newspapers and expired condiments, you're deviant; if it's filled with old gas pumps that cheesy chain restaurants will restore and display for their goggle-eyed customers, you're a savvy investor and arbiter of value. One show highlights the market gems and downplays the mountains of undesirable junk, while the other reverses this, focusing mostly on the valueless junk and the toll its exponential growth takes on the hoarders and their loved ones. In the special reflective recap episode, *American Pickers: Off the Road*, Mike is asked to respond to the question sometimes asked of him: what's the difference between your show and *Hoarders*? "People on our show are *proud*," he declares. If the predominant sentiment expressed by the junk dealers in *American Pickers* is pride, the atmosphere of *Hoarders* presents the towering midden-heaps of domestic America as a source of shame. In the former, dirty mountains of objects are the records of a life of adventure, travel, curiosity, hobbies, interests, or benign accumulation; while in the latter, the people living under the shadow of their disorders are hard cases: antisocial, damaged people. Massive trash bins and psychiatric counselors are

FIGURE 19

brought in, and everyone starts chucking in the vast majority of the offal from the fetid houses as its owners look on in obsessive-compulsive anguish. If Baudrillard was right to suggest that "consumption is irrepressible, in the last reckoning, because it is founded upon a *lack*," shows like *Hoarders* are designed to diagnose that lack by lingering over the terrible wastes buried in the cramped houses of the desperate and deranged.

One class of hoarders is adept at policing its garbage, while the other fails. One show imagines perfect markets where the new and the old circulate side by side in a culture of endless repurposing and profit-generating (value without use), and the other imagines a world of properly adjusted individual mentalities, which are needed in order for the world of consumption to continue without revealing too much about its own built-in schizoid relationship to production, accumulation, and value. In *American Pickers*, the "lack" is the modern condition of low-quality goods that can only be remedied by resurrecting the noble past embodied in talismanic objects of value, whereas in *Hoarders* and its related types of shows, the lack is a psychological affliction, and addiction to trash that serves as the symptom of social awkwardness or mental illness. The irony is that one of the things that makes the hidden treasures unearthed on *American Pickers* valuable now is that they were once seen as unvaluable, and thus discarded—in just the way that the detritus of the hoarders is seen as valueless. Things that have survived the scrap heap are valuable in part because so many other objects of its kind found their way to the scrap heap. Both *American Pickers* and *Hoarders*, then, depend for their meaning on a cultural logic of trashability. *Hoarders* suggests that the proper place for all of this—all of it, and quickly—is the garbage heap, while *American Pickers* suggests that the proper place for all of this is anywhere other than the garbage, because that's where most of its companions already ended up.

Is it possible to read the human subjects that populate shows like *Hoarders* as something other than merely psychiatric problem cases? Far more immense and consequential acts of wastage don't receive this kind of attention and scorn, and certainly not this pathological eye. But why? Industries pile up astonishing amounts of waste as the mere cost of doing business, as does the average modern consumer, throwing out his seven pounds of trash each day. But those who live among their filth, those who reject the false concept of Away, are the ones cast as aberrant. They are diagnosed, mocked, or subjected to our armchair analysis. But of course it's those of us who indulge in the Away-fantasy who are the real deviants: not from social norms, but from truth. At the very least we can say that hoarders hold on to their own garbage rather than outsource its storage. The fact that they themselves would not describe it as trash is less consequential than the fact that, as Edward Humes notes, hoarders perform "a kind of public service," because they let us see what our true legacy looks like. Unlike the cheap spectacle these hoarders provide, most of us hoard our waste in outsourced landfills instead of our own living rooms, kitchens, and yards. Shows like *Hoarders* reveal that those of us who do the seemingly normal and healthy thing of dumping our mountains of trash into unseen dumpsites are in an equally unsavory position where the question of waste is concerned. The hoarder's lairs constitute an alternative space to the pristine, or only mildly messy, domiciles in which most of its TV audiences live their daily lives, and feel themselves to be of sounder mind.

Hoarders is thus in part about our cultural habit of attempting to regulate and normalize desire; about the dangers of manufactured desires run amok; about the perceived need for finding the happy medium of consumption and accumulation in a world that insists on it to the full limits of one's health and well-being. It is as if the hoarder has broken some unspoken covenant with the way we are supposed to relate to time, value, and objects. Beneath the rhetoric of obsession, compulsion, and mental and social crisis, what is meant to be most alarming to the viewer is the colonization of living space by the overwhelming force of accumulated garbage. The home has become a storage shed, and the business of enjoying the pleasures of one's more properly balanced modern home is disrupted here by the intrusion of too much enjoyment, too much indulgence in desires that have spoiled, that have transformed from dreams of possession to claustrophobic nightmares. The cultural logic of hoarding is that the opposite of enjoyment is too much enjoyment. Hoarding is the name we give to a particularly acute species of storage panic in the era of low-quality, low-cost goods, where our inability to reign in our desires for things exceeds our ability to house and organize and demonstrate use or value in them. Like the Collyer brothers buried under their own detritus, or the women of *Grey Gardens*, the hoarder has turned her back on a society that has given her an endless supply of objects to turn away with. It is no surprise to hear the more famous or affluent of hoarders described as merely eccentric, because it reminds us that accumulation is not bad (it's good and necessary, we're told!), but that it's outside the norm, off-center. In a society organized around conspicuous consumption the worst sin of all is to be someone other than Goldilocks—someone who either drowns himself and his mania in mountains of trash or someone who lives like the equally suspicious Spartan hermit, living off the grid, uninterested in phones or TV or internet, unconcerned about fashions and news and trappings. Like so much of the other pseudo-reality TV we consume, *Hoarders* and its variants allow their viewers the opportunity to express a vague empathy while trafficking in the salacious voyeurism that lets us (as we gaze at the commercial interruptions on our flat-screens) define ourselves in opposition to the pathological cases we find so compelling to gawk at from afar. Whether we realized it before or not, our waste objects must achieve a homeostasis with the clean and desirable objects of our lives. We want to be sure we are not being buried alive by the wrong sorts of things.

FIGURE 20

8 LAKE CARBAMAZEPINE

In the *Blickling Homilies of the Tenth Century*, we read of the sorrowful man who abandoned his "contemplation of the dust" and turned away from the affairs of the world. The thousand-year-old word for this contemplation of the dust, or "dust-spectacle," is *dustsceawung*. I can only imagine that a person living five hundred years before Shakespeare and Robert Burton must have felt—as those of their time did, and as we do—that the words we use too often feel inadequate to the feelings or ideas they attempt to describe. But from the vantage point of the twenty-first century, *dustsceawung* seems to carry with it something of the wistful, brown-gray heaviness that I feel when I think of the modern wastes that we have made.

For years the Great Lakes have been absorbing tons of residual chemicals from our flushed pharmaceuticals, their waters filling up with all manner of the waste remnants of synthetic compounds, including contaminants that were once part of many people's anti-depressant drug regimens. The most common of these chemicals in the lake is carbamazepine. A mood-stabilizer, carbamazepine is often used to treat people suffering from bipolar disorder, attention-deficit disorder, post-traumatic stress disorder, mania, and depression, especially in cases where the more commonly prescribed lithium is not sufficient. One of the many side effects of lithium and its related classes of drugs is dehydration. (Think of this and then spare another thought for all those empty water bottles piling up everywhere we turn.) The Great Lakes constitute a natural body of water that has become, in effect, an enormous pharmaceutical cocktail filled with the detritus of drugs designed to help us endure many of the terrible realities of our moment and ourselves, an immense inland ocean of anti-depressant byproducts, containing the chemical offal of our anxious, terrified, medicated age. Surely there are also some old collapsed monsters half-buried at the bottom of those lakes, and enigmatic bits of drift littering their shores, waiting to be pondered and discarded by some roaming modern philosopher. But now even the water itself is equally inscrutable to us. We cannot even say what the thing we call water actually is anymore. You cannot tell by looking where the water ends and where the waste we've dumped inside it begins. If there is a more quintessentially modern wasteland than this, I cannot fathom what it would be.

ACKNOWLEDGMENTS

nstead of withholding mention of my wife until the very end, I want to thank her now. Olivia has been the single most amazing person I have ever had the good fortune to know, and it is important that I acknowledge just how incredible she is any time I have the opportunity to do so. Without her, so many things—this book the least among them—would not be possible, and I cannot even begin to express in words just what an extraordinary person she is.

I also want to acknowledge everyone in the editorial community who helped bring this humble book into existence and make it much better than it was: Chris Schaberg, Ian Bogost, Susan Clements, Haaris Naqvi, Mary Al-Sayed, Kaiya Knox, Erin Little, and Alice Marwick, all of whom are talented, patient, accommodating, and indefatigable workers and human beings.

When I asked three of my favorite writers—Jeff Vandermeer, Leslie Jamison, and Alexander Chee—if they'd consider reading this book and maybe also writing some brief comments about it for blurbing purposes, each of them shocked me by instantly saying yes. Without even having seen what they ending up thinking about this thing (I'm typing this manuscript right now, so I have no clue at this moment in time what they'll think), I'm still going to acknowledge them for their kindness in the past and their possible kindness and attention to the book in the future.

A special thanks to the staff of the New York Public Library, where I worked on large chunks of the drafts of this book in small, windowless rooms while the opulent Rose Main Reading Room remained off-limits, as plaster rosettes fell from its ornate ceiling. Debris happens, and deadlines remain. I also wrote important bits and pieces of this book at various locales around the city—among them De Robertis Pasticceria in the East Village and Café Edison in midtown—that have already closed and begun their slow fade into oblivion, as the city's old haunts, so conducive to forms of thought and writing that don't seem to bubble up as forcefully as they do in the newer and sleeker spaces, gradually disappear. This seems like something that should be acknowledged.

My community of friends, colleagues, acquaintances, and interlocutors on Twitter, currently the only social media outlet I can abide, have also been invaluable to my process, in direct and indirect ways: supplying links, leads, ideas, and notions, and sometimes just serving as a useful counterforce to whatever unproductive tendencies the book in progress was sometimes drifting toward. There are too many of them to name, but they are out there to be found, and my work and life are much better for having them in them.

I have encountered many useful teachers along the way, both in and out of school settings, but two of the most directly relevant to the existence of this book are Hank Webb and Mark Hawkins, who opened their home to a teenage kid from the sticks and introduced him to worlds of art, literature, culture, sociality, and friendship that he had not known existed in those forms. Anything I've written in the decades since I was fortunate enough to meet them has been shaped in large or small ways by their profound but gentle influence. This book is meant in part as a tribute to Mark and the other loved ones who were once here but now are no longer here, and whose living presence as dear friends and beloved family members persists now only in memory, where so much less decays.

Initially I wasn't going to include an acknowledgments page at all, mostly because I felt that it would be inadequate and incomplete, and I had planned to do something less public and more personal by expressing my gratitude to everyone individually instead. But then a conversation about the subject with Alison Kinney, Alyssa Harad, and Jeffrey Jerome Cohen convinced me that leaving out an acknowledgments page was not all that wonderful an idea, even if my reasons for wanting to do so seemed sound. So this page exists because of their helpful intervention. They reminded me that friends and communities matter, and that acknowledging them matters. In fact, they seem to matter most to those of us who still have the most to learn.

LIST OF
ILLUSTRATIONS

All images courtesy Library of Congress Prints & Photographs Catalog.

BIBLIOGRAPHY

Alexander, Leigh. "The Unearthing." May 30, 2014. Web.

Bataille, Georges. *The Accursed Share: An Essay on General Economy. Volume One: Consumption*. New York: Zone Books, 1988.

Baudrillard, Jean. *The System of Objects*. London: Verso, 2006.

Bauman, Zygmunt. *Wasted Lives: Modernity and its Outcasts*. Cambridge, MA: Polity Press, 2004.

Bienkowski, Brian. "Prescription Drugs Entering the Great Lakes at Alarming Rate." *Ecowatch.com*. November 27, 2013. Web.

Bullard, Robert. *Dumping in Dixie: Race, Class, and Environmental Quality*. 3rd ed. Boulder: Westview Press, 2000.

Calvino, Italo. *Invisible Cities*. San Diego: Harcourt Brace Jovanovich, 1978.

Calvino, Italo. "La Poubelle Agréée." *The Road to San Giovanni*. New York: Pantheon, 1993.

Chen, Angus. "Rocks Made of Plastic Found on Hawaiian Beach." *Science* (June 4, 2014). Web.

D'Agata, John. *About a Mountain*. New York: W. W. Norton, 2011.

Debatty, Régine. "Don't call it ruin porn, this is Ruin Lust." *we-make-money-not-art.com*. April 11, 2014. Web.

Delany, Samuel R. "On *Triton* and Other Matters: An Interview with Samuel R. Delany." *Science Fiction Studies* 52, no. 7, part 3 (November 1990). Web.

Dick, Philip K. *Do Androids Dream of Electric Sheep?* New York: Ballantine Books, 1996 [1968].

Doctorow, E. L. *Homer & Langley*. New York: Random House, 2009.

Douglas, Mary. *Purity and Danger: An Analysis of the Concepts of Pollution and Taboo*. London: Ark Paperbacks (Routledge & Kegan Paul), 1984 [1966].

"ESA Space Ferry Moves Space Station to Avoid Debris." *European Space Agency*. November 4, 2014. Web.

Eugenides, Jeffrey. "Against Ruin Porn." *Boat Magazine* 2 (March 27, 2014). Web.

Fiennes, Sophie. *The Pervert's Guide to Ideology*. London: Zeitgeist Films, 2012.

Garber, Megan. "A Little Ship Just Saved the International Space Station." *The Atlantic* (November 6, 2014). Web.

Gero, Joan M. "Genderlithics: Women's Roles in Stone Tool Production." In *Engendering Archaeology: Women and Prehistory*, edited by Joan M. Gero and Margaret W. Conkey. Oxford: Basil Blackwell, 1991, 163–93.

Hastorf, Christine A. "Gender, Space, and Food in Prehistory." In *Engendering Archaeology: Women and Prehistory*, edited by Joan M. Gero and Maragret W. Conkey. Oxford: Basil Blackwell, 1991, 132–59.

"Hedging on Stability: Reality Goes Speculative." *Friends of the Pleistocene*. August 10, 2013. Web.

Hildebrandt, William R. and Kelly R. McGuire. "A Land of Prestige." In *Contemporary Issues in California Archaeology*, edited by Terry L. Jones and Jennifer E. Perry. Walnut Creek, CA: Left Coast Press, 2012, 133–52.

Hirsch, Steven. "Gowanus: Off the Water's Surface," 2014. Web.

Humes, Edward. *Garbology: Our Dirty Love Affair with Trash*. New York: Avery, 2013.

Inaba, Jeffrey/C-Lab. "Trash Mandala." 2008. Web.

Jackson, Thomas L. "Pounding Acorn: Women's Production as Social and Economic Focus." In *Engendering Archaeology: Women and Prehistory*, edited by Joan M. Gero and Maragret W. Conkey. Oxford: Basil Blackwell, 1991, 301–28.

James, William. *The Varieties of Religious Experience* New York: Library of America, 1987. 1–478.

Jones, Terry L. and Kathryn A. Klar. *California Prehistory: Colonization, Culture, and Complexity*. Lanham, MD: Altamira Press, 2010.

Jordan, Chris. "*Midway: Message from the Gyre*." Web.

Kohler, Chris. "How Obsessed Fans Finally Exhumed Atari's Secret Game Graveyard." *WIRED* (April 29, 2014).

Leary, John Patrick. "Detroitism." *Guernica*. January 11, 2011. Web.

Liboiron, Max. "Waste as Profit & Alternative Economies." *Discard Studies*. July 9, 2013. Web.

Macaulay, Rose. *Pleasure of Ruins*. New York: Barnes & Noble, 1996 [1953].

McNeill, J. R. *Something New Under the Sun: An Environmental History of the Twentieth-Century World*. New York: W.W. Norton, 2000.

Madrigal, Alexis C. "Detroit 'Ruin Porn' from a Drone." *The Atlantic* (July 12, 2012). Web.

Michel, Lincoln. "Lush Rot." *Guernica*. March 17, 2014. Web.

Miller, Benjamin. *Fat of the Land: Garbage in New York—The Last Two Hundred Years*. New York: Four Walls Eight Windows, 2000.

Morris, Richard. *Blickling Homilies of the Tenth Century*. Web.

Morton, Timothy. *Hyperobjects: Philosophy and Ecology after the End of the World*. Minneapolis: University of Minnesota Press, 2013.

"Mount Everest litter targeted by Nepalese authorities." *The Guardian*. March 3, 2014. Web.

Myles, Eileen. "Spoilage." PEN World Voices Festival. 2013. Web.

New Mexico Energy, Minerals and Natural Resources Department. "Waste Isolation Pilot Plant Transportation Safety Program." Web.

Nixon, Rob. *Slow Violence and the Environmentalism of the Poor*. Cambridge, MA: Harvard University Press, 2013.

Orland, Kyle. "Digging up meaning from the rubble of an excavated Atari landfill." *Ars Technica*. April 27, 2014. Web.

"Paying Attention in an Age of Distraction: On Yves Citton's *Pour un Écologie de l'Attention*." *Unemployed Negativity*. November 16, 2014. Web.

Peters, Adele. "See the devastated landscape of the Alberta Tar Sands from 1,000 Feet Above." *Fast Company* (May 19, 2014). Web.

Pezzullo, Phaedra. *Toxic Tourism: Rhetorics of Pollution, Travel, and Environmental Justice*. Tuscaloosa, AL: University of Alabama Press, 2007.

Royte, Elizabeth. *Garbage Land*. New York: Back Bay Books, 2006.

Schiller, Jakob. "Can Detroit's Architectural Past Inspire It to Claw Its Way Back to Greatness?" *WIRED* (29 July 2013). Web.

Sebald, W. G. *On the Natural History of Destruction*. New York: Random House, 2003.

Sebeok, Thomas A. *Communication Measure to Bridge Ten Millennia*. BMI/ONWI-532, for Office of Nuclear Waste Isolation (1984). March 13, 2014. Web.

Shiplett, Julia. "What Ruin Porn Means to a City Rebuilding Itself." *Medium*. December 3, 2013. Web.

Slenske, Michael. "A Brooklyn Photographer Found a Secret 'Mother Lode' of Psychedelic Beauty in Filth of the Gowanus Canal." *New York* (November 12, 2014). Web.

Smithson, Robert. "A Tour of the Monuments of Passaic, New Jersey." *Artforum* (December 1967) 52–7.

Stallybrass, Peter. "Marx's Coat." In *Border Fetishisms: Material Objects in Unstable Spaces*, edited by Patricia Spyer. New York: Routledge, 1998, 183–207.

Trauth, Kathleen M., Stephen C. Hora, and Robert V. Guzowski. "Expert Judgment on Markers to Deter Inadvertent Human Intrusion into the Waste Isolation Pilot Plant." *Sandia Report* (SAND92 – 1382/UC – 721). Prepared by Sandia National

Laboratories for U.S. Department of Energy, November 1993. March 12, 2013. Web.

Tringham, Ruth E. "Household with Faces: The Challenge of Gender in Prehistoric Architectural Remains." In *Engendering Archaeology: Women and Prehistory*, edited by Joan M. Gero and Maragret W. Conkey. Oxford: Basil Blackwell, 1991, 93–131.

"The Trouble With Tribbles." *Star Trek* episode, NBC, 1967.

Valéry, Paul. "Eupalinos, or The Architect." In *Selected Writings of Paul Valéry*. New York: New Directions, 1964.

Villagran, Lauren. "WIPP probe: Emails raise new questions." Web.

Wall-E. Walt Disney Studios, 2008.

Wallace, David Foster. *Infinite Jest*. New York: Little, Brown, 1996.

Wanenchak, Sarah. "The Atemporality of 'Ruin Porn': The Carcass & the Ghost." *Cyborgology*. Web.

"What Will the Constellations Look Like in 50,000 Years?" *Discovery* (December 12, 2012). Web.

Williams, Gilda. "It Was What It Was: Modern Ruins." In *RUINS*, edited by Brian Dillon. Cambridge, MA: The MIT Press, 2010, 94–9.

"WIPP Radiation Release." Southwest Research and Information Center. March 5, 2014. Web.

Wolfe, Gene. *The Book of the New Sun*. New York: Simon and Schuster, 1980.

Yukimura, Makoto. *Planetes: Volume I*. Los Angeles: TOKYOPOP, 2003.

Zanisnik, Bryan. "Beyond Passaic." *Triple Canopy* 15. December 1, 2011. Web.

Zielinski, Luisa. "Capturing the 'Ruin Porn' of Berlin." *Nautilus* 7. November 7, 2013. Web.

INDEX

Page references for illustrations appear in *italics*.